The Soul & Spirit Of A Hummingbird

by

LESLIE RENEE BRISCOE-ANDREWS

A 52 week faith based devotional and prayer journal for the woman seeking a sacred space for reflection, growth and discovery on her journey to empowerment and resilience.

PUBLISHED BY TDR BRANDS INTERNATIONAL AND LEGACY PUBLISHING COORDINATORS

This devotional and journal is dedicated to those who have a heart for God and are seeking His voice, direction, and guidance. It is meant for those who want to walk in excellence and become the best version of themselves. The path to growth is not pretty; it is hard work and filled with difficult choices and truly taking the time to explore who you really are at the core. I'm sure you may be wondering why I refer to this as a "joy" journal. It's because joy is a journey—an ongoing process and an indicator of your spiritual health. It takes self-reflection and personal work to get there. One of my favorite quotes reads, "Joy is a decision, a really brave one, about how you are going to respond to life." You can't achieve it without God.

The pressures of life make it hard for us to carve out time for ourselves—time to get focused on our priorities and even time to count our blessings. As a professional, wife, mother, daughter, sister, and friend, I find myself wearing many hats and juggling myriad priorities. My roles in life have also changed along the way. Divorced and a single mom for over a decade, I am now remarried and blending a family. Along the way, I have found some things that work for me, that have allowed me to embrace the heart of who I am in Christ and to allow that Leslie to be known to the world. For me, it starts with grounding myself in the Word of God. I also believe in the power of prayer and the words we digest into our daily thinking. Reflection is also critical, and I find journaling to be a powerful tool in which to absorb and process my thoughts, responses, and feelings about what is going on in my life.

In sharing these weekly focus scriptures, I hope to give you a quick and easy tool to begin each week with purpose and focus. I promise setting aside this sacred time each week will not only give you clarity as you move into your week, but will ground you first in the word and move you into reflection and gratitude. Gratitude is indeed the root of joy, and isn't that ultimately what we are all seeking? Join me each week as we unpack a focus Scripture through Leslie's Lens—my personal reflection on the Word—along with a word of the week (WOW). This WOW is described figuratively, but then I ask you to look at it further, in relation to the Scripture, and in how you can implement it into your week. There are also several prompts to keep you focused on your priorities, mindful of your progress, and grateful for God's goodness! Every day is indeed a gift!

Letter to the Reader

So glad to have you join me on this journey to joy! I'm Leslie, and my faith is at the core of who I am! Spreading joy is not only what I do, but who God created me to be! Connecting those dots and embracing that truth has brought me to a true place of self-acceptance, peace, and authenticity. This journal is a result out of that truth, the work done to peel away the layers of who the world wanted me to be versus who God needs me to be. That work is never done; it is an ongoing process as we seek to improve and live a life according to God's plan. I am beyond excited to share this with you!

Operating in excellence and integrity are core values that I strive to emulate in everything I do. My passion to share the love and light of God was born out of my journey, a journey with tons of ups and downs, successes and failures, heartbreak and betrayals, but also filled with immense gratitude for the lessons learned, my family and friends, the people God sent to teach and guide me, the experiences, the joy, and those little things that make our hearts happy. One of my biggest lessons is found in the following quote, "Joy empowers you to rise above any circumstance." We can choose to crumble when life gets hard or we can rise up, dust off our knees, and trudge forward—scrapes and all. We truly can do "All things through Christ who strengthens us" (Philippians 4:13). We just have to trust and believe. Never stop believing!

That is something else you need to know about me. I am an eternal optimist, always believing in God, the people I love, the people I work with and encounter, and most importantly believing in myself. I love to cheer people on, to help them dig deep and find that strength we all have inside to push through and achieve our goals. Sometimes we just don't see it or have the confidence to tap into it. That is when we rely on our angels and the Lord to see us through.

So, friend, I am happy to meet you and pray you can use this labor of love as a tool toward achieving the personal and spiritual growth you may be seeking. There is no magic wand to fix our broken lives; we just have to know and understand that we are all a beautiful work in progress. God's masterpieces, perfectly imperfect, but precious in His sight.

In His love,

Leslie

My Prayer for You

My dearest heavenly Father, in the name of Jesus – I come to You as humbly as I know how – asking You to bless each and every person beginning this devotional journey with us. I pray the words and thoughts You poured into my heart touch them and bless them in a mighty way.

Help each and every participant glean Your wisdom and insight, and may they each take it with them in their daily lives. Allow these scriptures and lessons to resonate and create deeper insight and understanding of Your Word. We all want to be more like You, and I ask that each of us walk in Your authority each and every day. We are children of the Most High and are fearless, covered, and uniquely anointed.

There is purpose in our lives, and we desire to walk in our grace. Help us to shine Your light and love in all that we say and do. It is our responsibility to perhaps be the only glimpse of God some people may encounter. Help us to build Your kingdom and be Your hands and feet. We ask that You prick our hearts to do all things in love and to show compassion and empathy to those in need. Lastly, I ask that You meet each person where they are; You know their hearts and their deepest dreams and desires. We give You all the glory, all the praise, and all the honor.

I ask these and other blessings in Your mighty, magnificent, and matchless name. Amen.

Week One:
I can do all things through Christ who strengthens me

PHILIPPIANS 4:13 (NKJV)

This is one of the first scriptures I taught my daughter—not only because it was concise and easy to remember for a young child, but because of the power it packs. Whispering this scripture to yourself can be so empowering. It leave you feeling ready and prepared to tackle whatever is at hand. I find myself reciting it before a potentially tough meeting, conversation, or whatever else I might face in a day. My daughter now says it before tests and projects. The fact that my daughter has learned this power truly makes my heart so happy. As parents, we want so badly to instill strong beliefs and values in our children. We walk a fine line though, because we also want them to be their own person. I try my hardest not to force my faith on my child but to live it so that she sees it as a living and breathing choice with great value. Life is not easier because we've chosen to follow Christ, perhaps even the opposite, but the peace we have in our hearts, knowing His way is the truth and the light, helps us along our journeys. This verse is a natural confidence booster that never gets old! Make it a part of your daily repertoire!

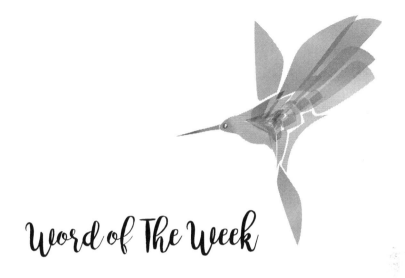

Word of The Week

EMBOLDENED

"Embolden," like Philippians 4:13, is quite powerful. It means having or giving the courage and/or confidence to do something or to behave in a certain way. Doesn't God do just that? He gives us the power and authority to walk boldly, to speak boldly, and to act boldly in His name! How will you allow the spirit of God to embolden you this week?

Shall we Pray?

Lord we come to you today first and foremost giving you thanks. Lord we are also coming to you asking boldly for some things in our life. You know our hearts and the things we only speak about in our secret places. You are a bold God and are not intimidated by the things we look at as difficult. There is truly nothing too hard for you and there are times we forget that in our day to day existence. Help us Lord, forgive us Lord for we are weak when you are strong.

Help us to put our faith fully in you and believe that you have the ability to make it so. Your will be done Father. We thank you in advance for all you are doing in our lives and celebrate the victories to come. God honors bold prayers because bold prayers honor God.

Listen to your heart

- **I feel:** _a little anxious_
- **I need:** _productivity_
- **I forgive:** _____
- **I celebrate:** _____
- **I release:** _____
- **I trust:** _____

The best thing about this week was

_____

_____

Me time—self care commitment

100 squats per day

back on isa

sabbath

_____

I was grateful for:

_____

_____

_____

_____

_____

_____

Set Your Mind Free

_____

_____

_____

_____

_____

_____

_____

_____

_____

_____

_____

_____

_____

_____

_____

_____

Just Imagine

Week two:
God is within her, she shall not fall

– PSALM 46:5 (NIV)

This scripture makes me feel fearless. Failure is just not an option for me. God is within me, and that is a superpower no one can take from me—and people and circumstances will indeed challenge you. They will also count you out! It reminds me of a conversation my ex-husband and I had one time about our marriage and strength. He suggested I did not have the strength to leave our marriage, that I was too nice and would not walk away or give up. He was right about my resolve to not give up but staying in that unhealthy relationship would have meant I was giving up on myself. I found the strength that is inside all of us and that God will give you when you ask Him to guide you. Remind yourself Whose you are and walk in bold confidence.

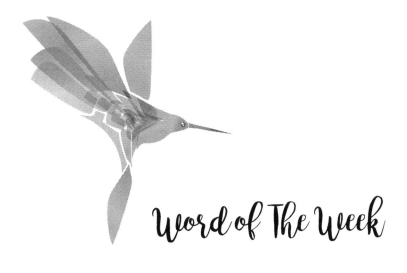

Word of The Week

FEARLESS

Simply stated, this means to be lacking of fear. Fearlessness, to me, became a mantra during a tough time in my life because, as the Bible says, if God is for us, who can be against us? (Romans 8:31) I realized I was allowing others' thoughts and opinions outweigh my thoughts, and more importantly, outweigh what God thought. God's Word is what matters. What challenge will you approach this week with a spirit of fearlessness? Walk in confidence knowing you are a child of the Most High!

Shall we Pray?

How excellent is thy name in all the earth. Oh gracious Father you are almighty and see and know all. There is nothing you are not prepared for and our faith remains solely in you. Help us Lord to walk in our faith and to put all fear aside. Help us to trust fully in your omnipotent power. You go before us in all we do. You prepare us and protect us. Help us to rest in this knowledge and walk boldly into our circumstances knowing you have a plan. You tell us that you have not given us a spirit of fear but one of power, love and sound mind. We are so very thankful and grateful for all that you are in our lives. We give you all the praise and lift our heads and hearts to you always.

listen to your heart

- I feel: _____
- I need: _____
- I forgive: _____
- I celebrate: _____
- I release: _____
- I trust: _____

The best thing about this week was

_____

_____

Me time—self care commitment

_____

_____

I was grateful for:

_____

_____

_____

_____

_____

It's time to daydream

_____

_____

_____

_____

_____

_____

_____

_____

_____

_____

_____

_____

_____

_____

Let your Mind Soar

Week three:
Now to him who is able to do immeasurably more than all we ask or imagine, according to his power that is at work within us, to him be glory in the church and in Christ Jesus throughout all generations, for ever and ever! Amen

EPHESIANS 3:20-21 (NIV)

Ahh! I love this scripture. It speaks to the limitlessness of God, even when we think we are asking big things of God, His answer can be even BIGGER! You can never out-bless or out-give our God! I used this scripture two years ago as my focus scripture for the year. I listed thirty brave prayers to help me notice how God orchestrated each one. While not all thirty were answered in that twelve-month period, quite a few were, and it blew my mind. God's power and His majesty are larger than life. We truly do not understand the magnitude of His glory. Even in the midst of COVID-19, which is still rampant at the time of this writing, He blesses us

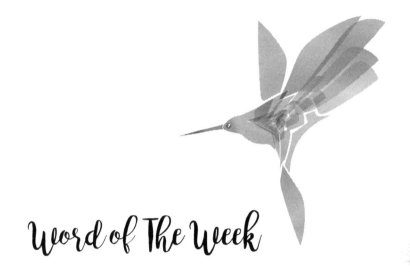

Word of The Week

LIMITLESS

"Without end limit or boundary." Try and digest that for a moment. God's love for us is limitless; His power is limitless. There is nothing He cannot do. All we have to do is ask and believe. Pray, believe, and receive. Focus on something you've been praying for—something that you know only God can do—and write it down and start praying it daily. Watch God work and blow your mind. He is limitless.

Shall we Pray?

Lord we come to you today first and foremost giving you thanks. Lord we are also coming to you asking boldly for some things in our life. You know our hearts and the things we only speak about in our secret places. You are a bold God and are not intimidated by the things we look at as difficult. There is truly nothing too hard for you and there are times we forget that in our day to day existence. Help us Lord, forgive us Lord for we are weak when you are strong.

Help us to put our faith fully in you and believe that you have the ability to make it so. Your will be done Father. We thank you in advance for all you are doing in our lives and celebrate the victories to come. God honors bold prayers because bold prayers honor God.

Listen to your heart

- I feel: _____
- I need: _____
- I forgive: _____
- I celebrate: _____
- I release: _____
- I trust: _____

The best thing about this week was

_____

_____

Me time – self care commitment

_____

_____

_____

I was grateful for:

_____

_____

_____

_____

_____

_____

Set Your
Mind Free

Just Imagine

Week four:
Surely your goodness and love will follow me all the days of my life and I will dwell in the house of the LORD forever

PSALMS 23:6 (NIV)

This verse brings me peace and reassurance that because of His love and protection, I will always be okay. When I look back over my life, He has shown me such grace and favor. Things that would have perhaps placed a chip on most people's shoulders have pushed me to be better. The loss of a sibling at a young age, divorced parents, multiple miscarriages, divorce—you name it. Life has happened, but I have not allowed it to dim my light. God's presence and movement in my life has always remained clear. Knowing I am a child of the Most High has given me an open outlook on life. It's given me the courage to do the hard work on myself and to welcome the good with the bad.

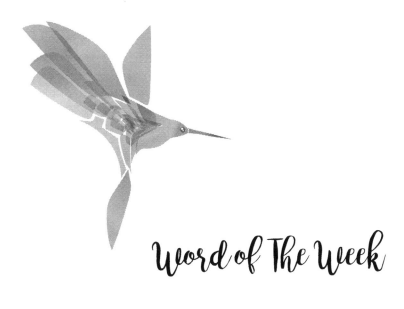

Word of The Week

REASSURANCE

This is the ability to remove doubts and fears. Isn't that just who God is? He has the ability to calm us when things are at their worst; to remind us that He is in control and that He will protect and guide us. What has God shown you recently to remind you that you are safe in His arms?

Shall we Pray?

Lord, we come to you today as humbly as we know how. Knowing that He who dwells in the secret place of the Most High shall abide under the shadow of the almighty! Lord you are our refuge and our fortress. You have shown us time and time again that you are with us even in those times when we feel alone. You are always there to wrap you loving arms around us to comfort us. Lord we are your children and we can come to you in good times and in bad.

There is nothing we can't share with you. As we go into a new week we take this reassurance with us. We will walk calmly into the week without anxiousness and without doubt. Knowing you go before us and that any trial is not meant to highlight our weaknesses but to strengthen us for the journey ahead. We ask these and other blessings in your mighty and matchless name.

listen to your heart

- I feel: _____
- I need: _____
- I forgive: _____
- I celebrate: _____
- I release: _____
- I trust: _____

The best thing about this week was

_____
_____

Me time – self care commitment

_____
_____

I was grateful for:

_____
_____
_____
_____
_____

It's time to daydream

_____

_____

_____

_____

_____

_____

_____

_____

_____

_____

_____

_____

_____

_____

_____

_____

Let your
Mind Soar

Week five:

I praise you because I am fearfully and wonderfully made; your works are wonderful, I know that full well

PSALMS 139:14 (NIV)

This verse just leaves me in awe – do you realize you are a masterpiece created uniquely by the Most High? So many times, we as women knock ourselves down and sell ourselves short. We compare ourselves to others and spend more time trying to emulate others than we do God. Comparison is the thief of joy, and you will soon realize it is a waste of energy. Learn to embrace who God made you to be. There is purpose in you as is. If He wanted you to be different, He would have made you that way. I tell myself all the time that I'd give anything to be a little taller – I stand a whopping 4'11, but have come to terms with the saying "good things come in small packages." God makes no mistakes, and He made you to be the unique and beautiful gift you are.

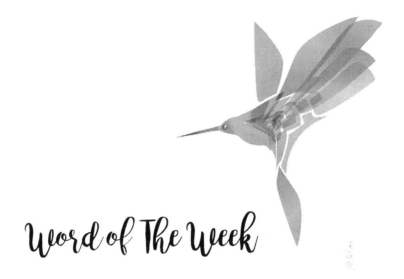

Word of The Week

MASTERPIECE

Masterpiece" is defined as a work of outstanding artistry, skill, or workmanship. We are God's masterpieces, His handiwork, and He knows every hair on our head and every fiber of our being. Embrace the unique gift of you. What is one thing you love about yourself? Focus on that this week!

Shall we Pray?

Our dearest heavenly Father – we balance so many things every day and many days we question our value and our significance. There are so many competing priorities pulling at us and our time that we often put ourselves on the bottom of our list. Help us Lord to see ourselves as you see us – help us to remember that we are perfect in your sight!. There is purpose in us and in our talents and gifts. Help us to see them in full light so that we appreciate what we bring to the table instead of questioning it. As we use this week to focus on the one thing we truly love about ourselves, help us to embrace this and own it.

When we make our strengths even stronger there is not time for us to even pay attention to what others may say are our weaknesses. Let us be renewed and refreshed and focus on what we know is our super power. Let us embrace it and walk fully in it. When we love ourselves wholly we show others how to love us and that in itself is a gift. We love you, we thank you and we give you all the honor.

Listen to your heart

- I feel: _____
- I need: _____
- I forgive: _____
- I celebrate: _____
- I release: _____
- I trust: _____

The best thing about this week was

_____
_____

Me time – self care commitment

_____
_____
_____

I was grateful for:

_____
_____
_____
_____
_____
_____
_____

Set Your
Mind Free

_____

_____

_____

_____

_____

_____

_____

_____

_____

_____

_____

_____

_____

_____

Just
Imagine

Week six:
Do not judge according to appearance, but judge with righteous judgement

JOHN 7:24 (NASB)

One of the lessons I've learned over the years is that we are not the judge! There is only one Judge, and He will resolve any and all issues in our lives. If we keep our hands and our mouths out of it, He will take care of it! Have you had situations where you felt you were either in the position of judging—or worse, being judged? I sure have. It does not feel good either, especially when you feel you are being judged by someone close to you who you feel "knows" you. Why are they questioning you or casting judgement on you or your situation? I had a close family member question my actions and challenge what I felt was my integrity. It hurt me deeply because I felt there was no grace being shown. Didn't this person love me unconditionally? I had always been there for them and felt I had not ever judged just loved them in spite of themselves. When I called it out to them, they did not see it that way at all, but I shared how it hurt me and made me feel. After some time, we looked back on the situation and they agreed that perhaps they have been quick to judge my situation without truly walking in my shoes. It's all perspective, but it starts with us not stressing over what others may believe to be true. God knows our hearts, and that is all that matters

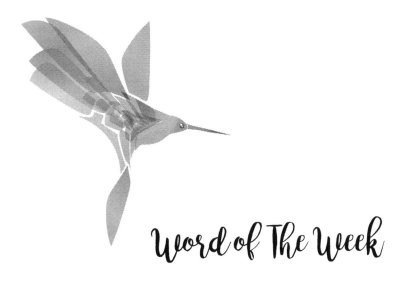

Word of The Week

JUDGEMENT

This is the ability to make considered decisions or come to conclusions. We are all guilty of judgement. It is natural for people to have biases based on their experiences or values. What we have to remember is that until we walk in another person's shoes we truly do not know or understand their story. What is the one thing or who is the one person you will refrain from judging this week?

Shall we Pray?

Lord we come to you asking you to give us an open mind and an open heart as we approach the coming week. Help us to see and hear the people in our lives and to do so without judgement or bias. We know that this is easier said than done but help us to understand it is not up to us to solve the world's problems or to identify the how, what or why. If we are true followers of your word we are to love one another as you have loved us. Unconditionally and without judgement. We are truly all more alike than we are different and if we would just take the time to hear each other's hearts we would see this clearly. Help us to do all things in love, to show grace and to have patience when our brother or sister say or do things differently than we do. We are all your children and you love each of us the same. Allow us to extend to other's the same grace we so readily desire. We are a work in progress but we commit this week to do and be better. In Jesus' name, amen.

listen to your heart

- I feel: _____
- I need: _____
- I forgive: _____
- I celebrate: _____
- I release: _____
- I trust: _____

The best thing about this week was

_____

_____

Me time—self care commitment

_____

_____

I was grateful for:

_____

_____

_____

_____

_____

It's time to daydream

_____

_____

_____

_____

_____

_____

_____

_____

_____

_____

_____

_____

_____

_____

_____

Let your Mind Soar

Week seven:
Trust in the LORD with all your heart and lean not on your own understanding

PROVERBS 3:5 (NIV)

There is an old saying that "father knows best," and I believe it to be true, but it is our Heavenly Father who knows what is best for us. The sooner we release control to Him, the better off we are. This is one of those verses I find myself reciting in my head when I'm having a day where nothing goes according to plan. I am a planner at heart and love a schedule and a to-do list. When the "unforeseen variables (as my husband calls them) happen, I've learned to pause and take a deep breath before getting bent out of shape. God has a reason for everything. Every one of our steps is ordered, and there is a plan. Even when it takes me off my plan, I have to trust His process. He's got us all in the palm of His hand

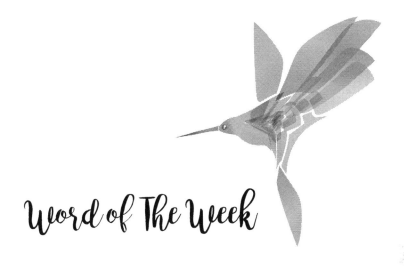

Word of The Week

TRUST

"Trust" is a firm belief in the reliability, truth, ability, or strength of someone or something. That is a small word with big meaning. How do we trust that the earth will keep spinning, the pilot to safely land the aircraft when we board an airplane, and that the plane will stay in the air, so why do we falter with fully trusting God? He shows us time and time again that He's got us. All we have to do is believe. What is the one thing that you've been wanting to trust God for? Leave it with Him and watch Him work it out for your good

Shall we Pray?

Lord, we come to you this week with the desire to fully place our trust in you. Not just some of the time but all of the time. We release the control and just place our burdens, cares, fears and worries at your feet. We know that you are still on the throne and you have proven to us over and over again just how much you hear our cries. We are taking this time to get clear and trust you to work your wonders. You know what it is that we need and we know that you will resolve it in your way not ours. Be with us if we become anxious this week and begin to question things. Doubt is a form of disbelief and we believe in you so we put our faith to the test and choose to trust in you always. We thank you in advance for all you are doing in our lives – amen.

Listen to your heart

- I feel: _____
- I need: _____
- I forgive: _____
- I celebrate: _____
- I release: _____
- I trust: _____

The best thing about this week was

_____

_____

Me time—self care commitment

_____

_____

_____

I was grateful for:

_____

_____

_____

_____

_____

_____

Set Your Mind Free

Just Imagine

Week Eight:
She who kneels before God can stand before anyone

ROMANS 8:31

This is a version of "If God is for us, who can be against us." To me, this is basically telling us not to worry about what others think or what they have to say about us. I am sure we are all guilty of doubting ourselves. I know I sure do. In my professional life, I have found that I am a heart-led leader where those around me may lead differently. At the end of the day, I get the necessary results, but there have been many situations in which my leadership style may have come into question. Why don't I just do it this way? Say it this way? Write it this way? Well, because I am me, and God made me who I am for a reason. When I operate fully in the gifts He has given me, I can never go wrong. We are perfect in His sight, and that is really all that matters. Please walk in the confidence the knowledge of this brings

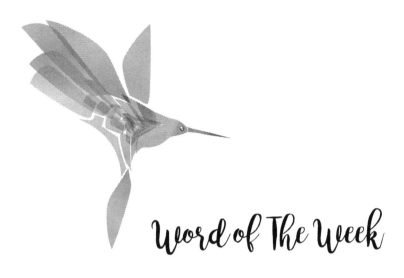

Word of The Week

CONFIDENCE

Confidence, in part, is the belief that one can rely on someone or something. Of course I have confidence in God, but what this verse gives me is confidence in who I am in God. Not only the confidence He instills in me but the power that confidence gives me, gives all of us. Whatever tough thing you may be facing this week—a meeting, doctor's appointment, phone call, etc.—keep this verse in mind and walk in the confidence only God can give us.

Shall we Pray?

Lord we ask that you bolster our confidence. Help us to remember that you go before us in all that we say and do. We are never alone and must learn to take dominion over any room or situation we walk into every day. We are your daughters and cannot take that lightly. The atmosphere should change when we arrive. Let our confidence be heard, felt and seen and not in an arrogant or overbearing way, but in a way that honors you. That makes other curious about our confidence and our demeanor. With you on our side we cannot lose and we are forever grateful for your love. Amen.

listen to your heart

- I feel: _____
- I need: _____
- I forgive: _____
- I celebrate: _____
- I release: _____
- I trust: _____

The best thing about this week was

_____

_____

Me time – self care commitment

_____

_____

_____

I was grateful for:

_____

_____

_____

_____

_____

_____

_____

It's time to daydream

Let your Mind Soar

Week nine:

Be strong and courageous. Do not be afraid or terrified because of them, for the LORD your God goes with you; he will never leave you nor forsake you.

DEUTERONOMY 31:6 (NIV)

Every day, when I get up, I feel like I have to put on my armor – I pray, sometimes meditate, and read my daily devotional or a passage of the Bible to get my mind and heart right for what the day will bring. Life can be crazy, and we are all juggling a ton of things—work, family, parenting, spouses, parents, and the list goes on. If I just go into my day unprepared, I find that my response to the inevitable surprises are not as strong as they should be. It makes sense though, doesn't it? If you have an exam and don't prepare for it by studying the information and preparing and reviewing your notes, ultimately your performance will suffer. It is the same with our lives. His word prepares us and shields us from whatever the enemy may have for us each day! Life can be a battle but when we rest in the fact that He's got us we can approach it with a smile.

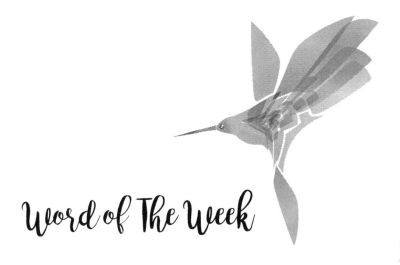

Word of The Week

COURAGEOUS

This word is defined as "brave, not deterred by danger or pain." The word "courageous" is more than an adjective to me; it is a physical element. Something I mentally arm myself with each day. I know I will need to it to deal with the unknowns of the day, and I will need it to stay true to who I am in Christ. It is easy to succumb to the ways of the world and not stand on the integrity and values I treasure. As you get dressed each morning, imagine you are putting on your courage along with your clothes, make-up, jewelry, and shoes. Make it a part of your daily wardrobe and your day.

Shall we Pray?

Courage my dear Lord, we ask you to continue to strengthen us and to give us the courage we need to not quit. We must be strong and ready each and every day for the battles in front of us. You have given us a secret weapon Lord to bolster our courage and that is love. When we lead in love and do all things with a spirit of love we truly show the true meaning of courage The focus is less on us and more on you which results in win-win situation for us all. You continue to be so very good to us and we continue to give you all the glory and all the honor. We thank you in advance for the many blessings, seen and unseen you are gracing us with and promise to unleash a spirit of courage this week as we move about our days.

Listen to your heart

- I feel: _____
- I need: _____
- I forgive: _____
- I celebrate: _____
- I release: _____
- I trust: _____

The best thing about this week was

_____
_____

Me time – self care commitment

_____
_____
_____

I was grateful for:

_____
_____
_____
_____
_____
_____
_____

Set Your
Mind Free

Just Imagine

Week ten:
May the God of hope fill you with all joy and peace in believing, so that by the power of the Holy Spirit you may abound in hope.

ROMANS 15:13 (ESV)

Do you remember being a child and believing with abandon that Santa Clause, the Tooth Fairy, and even the Easter Bunny were real? That is the same level of intensity that we should pour into our belief that the Father reigns. I have always loved fairy tales and the dream of "happily ever after." Even as an adult, I have not lost the ability to dream and believe. I think as we mature, it is so easy to lose the innocence of our childhood and the true ability to believe and to do so unconditionally. Life, however, is a test, and I can say that I have had my share of opportunities to put this belief to the test. One such time was the birth of my daughter. She came into the world at 28 ½ weeks, more than ten weeks early. The doctors were quick to tell me all the things that could potentially be wrong with her. Cognitive issues, slow development, learning disabilities, and many physical impairments. If this was God's will, it would be just fine, but I believed God's promise that this child was answered prayer and that in spite of all her health issues, she would not only be healthy, but not one of the conditions they claimed would come to pass. It got so bad at one point that the nurses asked my sister if I was hearing them. Every time they talked, asked me to sign a form, I just started to pray. I believed she would be healthy and that she would thrive—and she did just that. This confidence to believe in Him should fill your hearts with joy, peace, and the knowledge that He will come again.

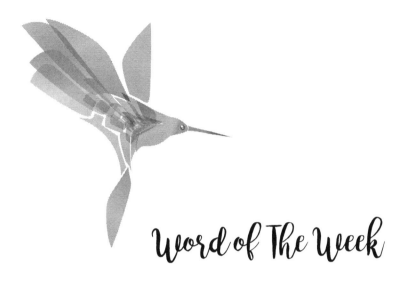

Word of The Week

— BELIEVE —

To believe is to accept something as true. Believing is a way of life for me. Even when those around me think I am naïve or a little strange, I tell them I like my world and that God never lets me down. Even when the outcome isn't exactly what I want, I trust and believe that His way is the only way. What is it that you are believing God for this week?

Shall we Pray?

Heavenly Father, we come to you today asking you to help our unbelief. Touch our hearts, our souls and our minds and give us the strength to trust in your will and your way. When all else fails, and when things look beyond our control, help us to look to the hills from whence our strength comes. You are the truth and the light and we must learn to believe in you with the same unwavering faith we had as children that Santa would come and visit and leave us our heart's desires. You Lord want nothing but the best for us. You want to fulfill all of our hopes, dreams and wishes. What we must learn to grasp is that many times what we "think" we want or need is really not what is best for us. You know what is best and we trust you to do your will in our lives. Let us embrace your love, guidance and protection and believe that you can and you will do it. Amen.

listen to your heart

- I feel: _____
- I need: _____
- I forgive: _____
- I celebrate: _____
- I release: _____
- I trust: _____

The best thing about this week was

_____
_____

Me time—self care commitment

_____
_____

I was grateful for:

_____
_____
_____
_____
_____
_____

It's time to daydream

_____

_____

_____

_____

_____

_____

_____

_____

_____

_____

_____

_____

_____

Let your Mind Soar

Week Eleven:
Rejoice in hope, be patient in tribulation, be constant in prayer

ROMANS 12:12 (ESV)

The power of prayer is real. I can remember asking my grandmother about praying when I was a little girl and asking how she could know God heard her. She told me I would learn, and boy was she right. Through trials and tribulations, happy times and sad times, I have developed my own prayer life and have experienced just how powerful prayer can be. Years ago, I started a prayer journal. At the beginning of the year, I choose a scripture that I pray consistently for my family. I also write down specific prayers that I have in my heart, and I ask family and friends to share their lists with me as well. I take this seriously, and I pray over these prayer requests daily. I also update the lists as prayers are answered or not answered. By placing a date by them, I am able to see the miracle of His work. This has been a huge faith-builder and has taught me how sacred praying for others is. Prayer is nothing more than a little chat with our Father—He hears us and cares about everything in our hearts and minds. Take it to Him and watch Him work!

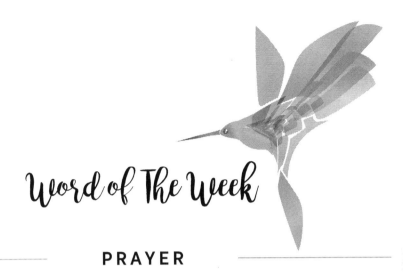

Word of The Week

PRAYER

Prayer is a solemn request for help or the expression of thanks addressed to God. Too often I think we complicate the definition of prayer. There is not a right or wrong way to pray. Prayer is simple; it is a conversation with God. How you choose to execute your conversation is up to you. It is unique to you. No one's way of praying is the same, and God does not expect it to be. He just wants us to commune with Him. How is your prayer life? Do you have one or do you need to develop one? Now is the time to start! Trust the process!

Shall we Pray?

Father, in the name of Jesus I ask you to please be with everyone this week as they prepare themselves for the challenges that lie before them. Lord I ask you to help them to know that they possess the most powerful weapon of all – it is free and simple and truly a gift. It is the power of prayer. Help them to realize the power of their words and that unleashing their innermost thoughts, fears, dreams and goals to you is exactly what you wish. You desire us to share with you and to trust that you are in control. You already know what we are thinking. All we need to do is lay it at your feet, you will take care of the rest. We are so grateful to you Lord and we thank you so much for loving and caring about our every need. We walk into this week with power, committed to having a chat with our Father as often as we need to. You are always present.

Listen to your heart

- I feel: _____
- I need: _____
- I forgive: _____
- I celebrate: _____
- I release: _____
- I trust: _____

The best thing about this week was

_____
_____

Me time—self care commitment

_____
_____
_____

I was grateful for:

_____
_____
_____
_____
_____
_____

Set Your Mind Free

Just
Imagine

Week twelve:
But the fruit of the Spirit is love, joy, peace, patience, kindness, goodness, faithfulness, gentleness, self-control

— GALATIANS 5:22 (ESV)

These nine beautiful attributes give us all the direction we need to live a life that is pleasing to Him. Some come more naturally to us than others, but each is equally important. Many times, we are the only glimpse of God's love some people will ever see. What impression do you want to leave with them? You can also think about it like this: how do you represent the kingdom of God? Are you doing a good job showing other's God's love, goodness, and grace? Christians give the church a bad rap. We are human of course and will make mistakes, but we have to take our roles seriously. We are here to help build the kingdom. To spread the good news. We have an accountability to God and to each other. He has given us the blue print to living in accordance with the Holy Spirit. How will you incorporate the fruit's of the spirit into your daily interactions this week? Which one(s) do you need to make a priority?

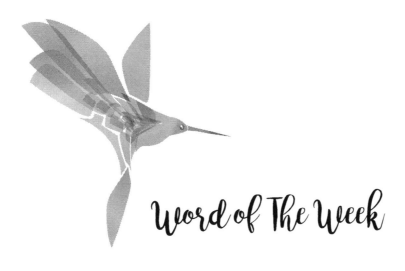

Word of The Week

INSTRUCTION

Instructions are detailed information telling how something should be done. Have you ever tried to put something together without following the instructions? Were you successful or were you left with screws and parts that had no home and an item that was not functioning properly? It is the same way for us—God supplies us with all the instruction we need to lead productive and fulfilling lives, but so many times, we leave out a portion of His instruction. Sure, we may get pretty far before we fail the test, but we need all of His instructions in order to be complete.

Shall we Pray?

Lord, we know that we are sinners and that we fail you miserably each and every day. We ignore your instruction and manipulate your word to fit our needs. Help us to do better and be better. Help us to be good stewards of your blessings and great examples of your word. People are watching and we must take our responsibility seriously. Of course we ask for grace as none of us are perfect but we know that we must strive to honor and fulfill your commandments. We are forever grateful to you and humbled by your love. Help us to show our gratitude and our loyalty to you by gracing those in our lives with these amazing principles – the fruit's of the spirit. Touch our hearts and give us direction as to what we need to focus on. Help us to hear your voice as it whispers to us where we are falling short. We promise to do our best to uplift your kingdom and show other's the love and grace you show us daily. Amen.

listen to your heart

- I feel: _____
- I need: _____
- I forgive: _____
- I celebrate: _____
- I release: _____
- I trust: _____

The best thing about this week was

_____

_____

Me time - self care commitment

_____

_____

I was grateful for:

_____

_____

_____

_____

_____

_____

It's time to daydream

_____

_____

_____

_____

_____

_____

_____

_____

_____

_____

_____

_____

_____

_____

Let your
Mind Soar

Week thirteen:
A joyful heart is good medicine, but a crushed spirit dries up the bones.

PROVERBS 17:22 (ESV)

Find the joy in everything, even when your circumstances point to the negatives in your life. Living a life full of joy breeds joy. There is more good in your life than there is bad; it's all about perspective. Dealing with all the challenges COVID-19 has brought our way is a perfect example. We have watched an unprecedented number of lives lost, suffering on all levels, job loss, increased suicide rates, domestic and child abuse cases and the list goes on. It is so easy to get bogged down in the negativity and the utter sadness that is all around us. But we have to pull ourselves up and out of despair and stay focused on His love for us. It is our job to spread that love, sharing it with anyone who asks. When we focus on the things we are grateful for in this life, we cannot help but allow joy to grow. Gratitude is indeed the root of joy.

Word of The Week

JOY

Great pleasure and happiness. Joy is the kind of happiness that is not dependent on what happens. It is rooted in the character and promises of God, not in external circumstances. Take a moment every day this week to identify what brings you joy. It can be as complex or simple as you want. I love having a hot cup of tea in the evening as I begin to wind down from the day. This very simple ritual has come to signify a little nugget of joy for me. I look forward to it daily and find myself exhaling and smiling inside out.

Shall we Pray?

Dear Lord, I ask you to help my sister look deep inside and find that one thing that brings her joy. The things that makes her heart happy. Help her to focus on this and realize that many times it is the little things that fill us the most. So much of our day is spent focusing on what has gone wrong, Lord help us to look at what has gone right. What surprised us today and made us smile unexpectedly? What gave us a sense of fulfillment as we prepared to wind down after a long day. Allow us to focus on this and realize there is so much more good in our life than bad. We have so much to be grateful for and we
Thank you for all you are doing in our lives. We give you all the praise, all the glory and all the honor Amen.

Listen to your heart

- I feel: _____
- I need: _____
- I forgive: _____
- I celebrate: _____
- I release: _____
- I trust: _____

The best thing about this week was

_____

_____

Me time – self care commitment

_____

_____

_____

I was grateful for:

_____

_____

_____

_____

_____

_____

Set Your Mind Free

Just Imagine

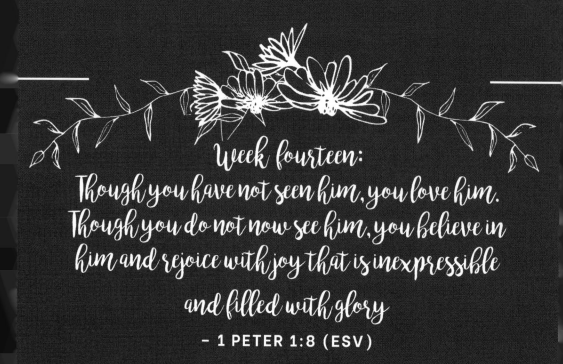

Week fourteen:
Though you have not seen him, you love him. Though you do not now see him, you believe in him and rejoice with joy that is inexpressible and filled with glory

– 1 PETER 1:8 (ESV)

Seeing is not always believing. I sometimes wonder what my faith looks like to an unbeliever. I am sure they question how I can so strongly believe when I've never seen God with my own two eyes. We breathe air that we cannot physically see but we trust that we can inhale and exhale every day; we walk by faith and not by sight. We must believe in the things we do not see. This is the true test of faith, and we will be rewarded in heaven. Have you ever had a situation where your faith came into question? Where you had to put it all on the line? I have had so many examples of this in my life, but the one that come to mind right away is when I found out I would be losing my job. My company was merging, and if I wanted to keep my job, I'd need to relocate to New York. My daughter was 2 ½ years old at the time, and it was out of the question for me. I had recently separated from my husband, and the one thing I had been counting on to keep us going was my income and the stability of my career. Well, my faith kicked in big time. People kept asking me what I was going to do. I had ninety days to get it figured out. What I knew for certain was that God had a plan. What it was, I had no idea, but I trusted that He would make a way for me. My prayer was not where, what, or when, but that the Lord provide me with a way to take care of my daughter and keep us roof over our heads and the bills paid. I didn't pray about the salary, the job—nothing. Just provision. Guess what? He provided. I had a job settled before my ninety-day timeframe came to a close. His mercies!

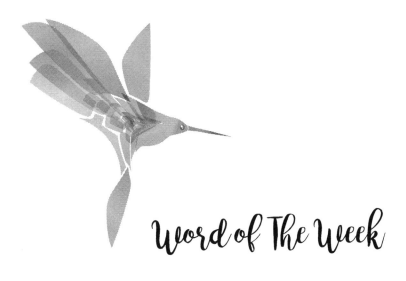

Word of The Week

FAITH

Faith is the complete trust, confidence, and belief in someone or something. It is the strong belief in God based on spiritual apprehension rather than proof. What are you trusting God with in your life right now? Are you relying heavily on your faith or questioning every twist and turn? Faith—not fear—should rule your heart. Let's start small and focus on one thing you are trusting God for. Let's put your faith to work and watch His faithfulness unfold.

Shall we Pray?

Oh Lord, our Lord how excellent is thy name in all the earth? Our faith and our trust is solely in you. We believe you to make it so and we release the spirit of fear, doubt and questioning that so easily comes into play when life gets hard. You have been there for us in the past and you will be there for us again today and tomorrow. We sit back in awe of your handiwork. The faith journey we are on is not exempt of trying times but what we know and believe to be true is that your timing is perfect. Your plan, executed in excellence and perfection. We are excited to see what is in store for us because our faith continues to teach us patience and trust in your abilities. We love you Lord and lift your name on high.

listen to your heart

- I feel: _____
- I need: _____
- I forgive: _____
- I celebrate: _____
- I release: _____
- I trust: _____

The best thing about this week was

_____

_____

Me time – self care commitment

_____

_____

I was grateful for:

_____

_____

_____

_____

_____

_____

It's time to daydream

_____

_____

_____

_____

_____

_____

_____

_____

_____

_____

_____

_____

_____

_____

_____

Let your Mind Soar

Week fifteen:
This is the day that the LORD has made; let us rejoice and be glad in it.

– PSALM 118:24 (ESV)

Whenever I read this scripture, I immediately think of Fred Hammond's song "This is the Day," and I'm energized and filled with joy. Every day is indeed a gift from above, and we should not waste it! Try listening to that song to get your day started! I promise you'll be ready for anything! During a difficult time in my life, I had this song on replay in my car. Getting up and out of the house some days was a struggle, but I had to rise above the struggles—if not for me, then for my little one. I would immediately push play as we backed down the driveway en route to her daycare. We'd both be singing it at the tops of our lungs, and by the time I dropped her off and was on my way to work, my entire mindset had changed. There is something good in every day and in every circumstance; all we have to do is seek it!

Word of The Week

GIFT

Gifts are tangible or intangible things given willingly to someone without payment. I immediately think of the fact that every day we open our eyes is a gift! I also can't help but think of the verse that every good and perfect gift comes from above! God loves us so much, He blesses us each and every day with gifts and blessings seen and unseen. So many times, we can be like spoiled children and not even appreciate the beauty in our lives. What can you identify in your life as a gift from above?

Shall we Pray?

Dear Lord, let us just say thank you. Thank you for the gift of our lives, for waking up this morning and for new mercies. Help us to know that there indeed is purpose in our lives. There are some who did not wake up today and you have given us another day to get it right. Help us to take this opportunity to not only give thanks to you but to show you how very much we love you by spreading the light and love of your word to others. Help us to be kingdom builders. Allow our light to shine so that others may be drawn to you. You have blessed each of us with gifts and talents and they are to be shared with others and meant to magnify you. We ask these prayers as humbly as we know how and we give you all the glory and honor. Amen

Listen to your heart

- I feel: _____
- I need: _____
- I forgive: _____
- I celebrate: _____
- I release: _____
- I trust: _____

The best thing about this week was

_____

_____

Me time – self care commitment

_____

_____

I was grateful for:

_____

_____

_____

_____

_____

_____

Set Your Mind Free

Just Imagine

Week sixteen:

Count it all joy, my brothers, when you meet trials of various kinds, for you know that the testing of your faith produces steadfastness. And let steadfastness have it's full effect, that you may be perfect and complete, lacking in nothing.

JAMES 1:2-4 (ESV)

I have found that my toughest times in life have produced a stronger, improved version of me. Our trials, while difficult, are not always a bad thing. Sometimes they lead to our biggest breakthroughs and blessings. We have to embrace the process, realizing that once we do, we will be fortified, lacking in nothing. I think so many times we as Christians think life should be easier—that we won't have to endure the tough times, but that could not be further from the truth. One thing I have learned along my journey is that sometimes the lessons are for me directly and sometimes the lesson may be for someone else. I have learned not to question it anymore. Instead of a "why me?" attitude, I've turned it into "why not me?" Perhaps God is using you specifically to deliver a message or lesson to someone who might only receive it from you. God works in mysterious ways, and His ways are not our own. You are not always going to understand it but we learn from it and grow and just keep getting better!

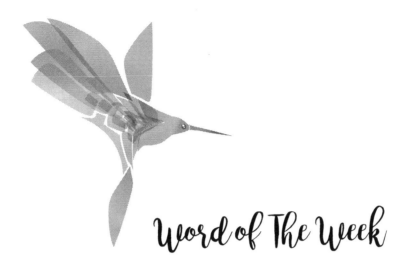

Word of The Week

BREAKTHROUGH

This is an unplanned and important discovery or development. Think back on a defining time in your life and how it changed you. What breakthrough resulted? What key lessons did you learn? Many times, our breakthroughs propel us to make necessary changes in our lives or to implement boundaries we've been "meaning" to add. Are there any breakthroughs in your life that you have not acted on? Now is the time—it is never too late!

Shall we Pray?

Our dearest Father, we ask you to be with us this week as we meditate on the breakthroughs or epiphanies we've had along our journey that we've not taken action on. If we don't move and make the necessary changes, we are destined to repeat the behavior and/or the lesson you are trying to correct or teach us. Help us to hear you clearly. Help us to be obedient when we hear from you. It can be so easy to talk ourselves out of the hard work that is sometimes necessary. Help us to be malleable and open to your will on our life. Not only are these lessons for us but for those around us. We are grateful that you love us enough to show us the way in which we should go. If I had one thousand tongues I would praise you with them all. We thank you and we honor you.

listen to your heart

- I feel: _____
- I need: _____
- I forgive: _____
- I celebrate: _____
- I release: _____
- I trust: _____

The best thing about this week was

_____

_____

Me time – self care commitment

_____

_____

I was grateful for:

_____

_____

_____

_____

_____

_____

It's time to daydream

_____

_____

_____

_____

_____

_____

_____

_____

_____

_____

_____

_____

_____

_____

Let your Mind Soar

Week seventeen:

For you shall go out in joy and be led forth in peace; the mountains and the hills before you shall break forth into singing, and all the trees of the field shall clap their hands.

ISAIAH 55:12 (ESV)

Having a spirit of joy is contagious! Sometimes the smile you share with someone is the only smile they may receive that day. We all have the ability to impact another person's life. And it is up to us to choose if that is going to be in a positive or negative way. Many days, I walk into the office and maybe my drive in was hectic, or I had a dis-agreement with my husband, or as life would have it, everything that could go wrong went wrong. I always think about what I bring with me—what baggage do I have with me? And I check it at the door. It is no one's fault on my team that I overslept, or my daughter had a nose bleed, I forgot to get gas and ended up behind every school bus imaginable, or that I happen to have a migraine today. What I bring with me, the spirit of joy or doom that I choose to focus on, impacts each person I encounter. It's up to me to choose wisely. Approach your day with this knowledge and spread some sunshine today!

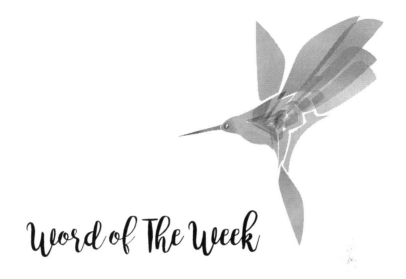

Word of The Week

SMILE

Share with someone a smile—an amused, pleased, or kind facial expression. A smile costs you absolutely nothing, but its benefit can reap huge rewards. How can you spread some sunshine this week? You'll be amazed at the positive response you receive and how it makes your own heart smile too!

Shall we Pray?

Dear Lord, we come to you as humbly as we know how seeking your guidance. Give us courage, strength and wisdom in all of the decisions looming in our lives. But Lord, help us to know that we are not in this thing alone. Sometimes we get so bogged down in the craziness of life that we forget the ultimate life-line we have in you. All we have to do is ask for your helping hand and you are right there for us, leading us to a place of safety and security. We are never alone, even when we are in so deep that we cannot see the light, we know you are there watching over us. We take your hand Lord and we ask you to lead us in all things. We rest in the safety of your loving arms and praise you for your unyielding love and support of us. Amen.

Listen to your heart

- I feel: _____
- I need: _____
- I forgive: _____
- I celebrate: _____
- I release: _____
- I trust: _____

The best thing about this week was

_____

_____

Me time – self care commitment

_____

_____

_____

I was grateful for:

_____

_____

_____

_____

_____

_____

Set Your Mind Free

Just
Imagine

Week Eighteen:
He reached down from high and took hold of me; He drew me out of deep waters.

– 2 SAMUEL 22:17 (NIV)

Never forget that God is still on the throne! Praise Him in the midst of your problems. He is the master of turning things around. I can remember, when I was contemplating my divorce, the feeling of desperation I had. I felt like I was failing miserably even though I had worked so hard to make my marriage work. I thought because I had prayed to God about it that He would just miraculously give me the answer: yes or no? But it wasn't that simple. It was not until I trusted not only Him but myself to take the first step towards reclaiming my life that He stepped all the way in. It was like He just needed to see me move, to show that I was stepping out in faith, and He literally took my hand and guided me through it all. With every decision, every move toward improving my life, I got stronger and more certain that this was the way I was supposed to go. This verse truly spoke to me during that confusing and difficult time in my life; I truly felt like He saved me from what felt like drowning.

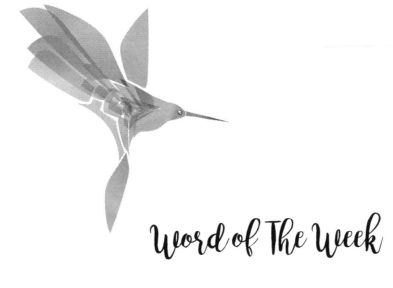

Word of The Week

RESOLVE

This is the firm determination to do something. My faith in God has given me resolve along with confidence and courage to walk boldly in what I believe He has for me. What concern or problem will you leave with God? What will you step away from and allow Him to settle for you?

Shall we Pray?

How excellent is thy name in all the earth. Oh gracious Father you are almighty and see and know all. There is nothing you are not prepared for and our faith remains solely in you. Help us Lord to walk in our faith and to put all fear aside. Help us to trust fully in your omnipotent power. You go before us in all we do. You prepare us and protect us. Help us to rest in this knowledge and walk boldly into our circumstances knowing you have a plan. You tell us that you have not given us a spirit of fear but one of power, love and sound mind. We are so very thankful and grateful for all that you are in our lives. We give you all the praise and lift our heads and hearts to you always.

listen to your heart

- I feel: _____
- I need: _____
- I forgive: _____
- I celebrate: _____
- I release: _____
- I trust: _____

The best thing about this week was

_____

_____

Me time—self care commitment

_____

_____

I was grateful for:

_____

_____

_____

_____

_____

_____

It's time to daydream

Let your
Mind Soar

Week Nineteen:
The LORD is my strength and my shield; in Him my heart trusts, and I am helped; my heart exults, And with my song I give thanks to Him

PSALM 28:7 (NASB)

Any time I feel weak or off-balance, I remind myself that the Lord is indeed my strength. I rely solely on Him to not only comfort me but to sustain me during my toughest times. We all have moments of weakness or times when we doubt ourselves, our abilities, our talents, all of it. Balancing a career, being a mom, and keeping a healthy marriage can be a challenge. I consider myself a recovering perfectionist—I like to do all things in excellence. That can be hard and cause unnecessary stress in my life as I work hard to be perfect in all of these areas. On those days when I am beating myself up for not being the best parent, wife, sister or friend, I think of this scripture and relax in knowing I do not have to face any of this alone. He is my rock, my shield, and my biggest cheerleader. In Him I trust!

Word of The Week

PROTECTION

Providing a barrier from suffering, harm, or injury. God is our ultimate protector. He only wants the best for us and loves us dearly in spite of ourselves. So many days, we have no idea what He has kept us from or protected us from. That car accident we passed by on the way to work? Have you ever thought "wow, I could have been involved in that had I left five minutes earlier"? It's all a matter of God's timing and His plans. Think about a time or a situation where you know God protected and kept you and give Him thanks! He is a fence!

Shall we Pray?

Precious Father, you not only go before us in all things but come behind us ensuring we are protected. Truly a fence around us we are sheltered in your arms. What comfort that brings my soul. In those moments when we become overwhelmed with life, help us to remember to rely on you. Help us to remember where our strength comes from and that we are not meant to do it all alone. We are your children and must remember that we are not in control, you are. You know all and see all – Alpha and Omega – you are worthy to be praised.

Listen to your heart

- I feel: _____
- I need: _____
- I forgive: _____
- I celebrate: _____
- I release: _____
- I trust: _____

The best thing about this week was

_____

_____

Me time – self care commitment

_____

_____

_____

I was grateful for:

_____

_____

_____

_____

_____

_____

Set Your Mind Free

Just Imagine

Week twenty:
For I know the plans I have for you, says the LORD. They are plans for good and not for evil, to give you a future and a hope.

JEREMIAH 29:11 (ESV)

- This verse brings me such hope and excitement about my future. He only wants what is best for us and His plans far outweigh ours. I continue to walk in great expectation of ALL He has for me! This verse makes me think about never limiting myself. It's never too late to rebuild, to update, or to change. We are all works in progress, getting better each and every day, and God's plans for us don't stop when we reach a certain age, get married, or have children. Our beautiful lives continue, and there is purpose in them. Never stop dreaming, planning, or hoping for more, or for something new and different. Never in a million years would I have thought that I would get remarried after being divorced/single for over a decade, but God—His timing is always right.

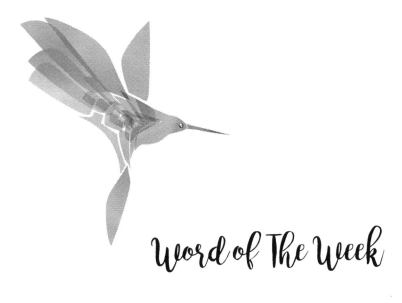

Word of The Week

EXPECTATION

Expectation is the strong belief that something will happen or be the case in the future. What dream or desire are you holding inside? Have you given up or put it aside because you think you are too old or too "this or that"? Bring it to the Lord and allow Him to do the work for you!

Shall we Pray?

Heavenly Father we are so excited and honored by all you are doing in our lives. We need your reminder that there are no expiration dates on your promises or on our prayers. You are in the business of making miracles happen and we claim each and every promise you have placed in our hearts. Help us to walk in great expectation every day of all that you are doing in our lives. We believe that there is purpose in our life and that your will bring it to fruition when the time is right. We know that your timing is perfect and we trust in you and in the process. We ask these and other blessings in your mighty and matchless name, amen.

listen to your heart

- I feel: _____
- I need: _____
- I forgive: _____
- I celebrate: _____
- I release: _____
- I trust: _____

The best thing about this week was

_____

_____

Me time – self care commitment

_____

_____

I was grateful for:

_____

_____

_____

_____

_____

_____

It's time to daydream

_____

_____

_____

_____

_____

_____

_____

_____

_____

_____

_____

_____

_____

Let your Mind Soar

Week twenty-one:
But let all who take refuge in you rejoice; let them ever sing for joy, and spread your protection over them, that those who love your name may exult in you

– PSALM 5:11

My love of God is endless and knows no boundaries. I take refuge in knowing He cares about me! As a Christian I feel it is my responsibility to share the love and light of God with others. There are so many ways to do this. You don't have to walk around hosting Bible studies—not that there is anything wrong with that! I try to live my life so that other's see God through my actions. I want people to be curious about God after an encounter with me. I pray that they see His light through my actions and in my words. My faith is at the core of who I am and spreading His message gives me joy.

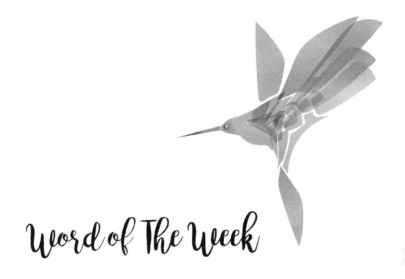

Word of The Week

ENDLESS

This adjective means having or seeming to have no end or limit. God's love for us has no end. It is the true meaning of agape love. The unconditional love that has no limit's. No matter what we do or say, He loves us, forgives us, and wants the best for us. Make a list of all the many ways He has shown you grace, mercy, and unmerited favor. I promise you: you'll be writing for quite some time.

Shall we Pray?

Heavenly Father, how can we not just drop to our knees and thank you at all times? Your grace and goodness overwhelm us and we are forever grateful for your love and care. We thank you from the depth of our souls and just continue to lift your name and glorify you in everything that we do. We ask that you use us Lord, use us to show other's your worth, your goodness and the many blessings you show us daily. Help us to spread the good word and to bring other's closer to you. We are the church and it is our duty to show other's your love. Help us to meditate this week on the many ways you continue to cover us and see us through our days. You protect us from danger seen and unseen and we humbly say thank you. In your name we pray -amen.

Listen to your heart

- I feel: _____
- I need: _____
- I forgive: _____
- I celebrate: _____
- I release: _____
- I trust: _____

The best thing about this week was

_____

_____

Me time - self care commitment

_____

_____

_____

I was grateful for:

_____

_____

_____

_____

_____

_____

Set Your Mind Free

Just Imagine

Week twenty-two:
For our heart is glad in him, because we trust in his holy name

PSALM 33:21 (ESV)

God is the center of my joy! I am filled with the gladness and peace that only He can give. I trust in Him fully, and this allows me to walk each day covered with a sense of understanding and protection that is hard to explain. So many days, we are hit with the challenges of life that can easily take us down, steal our joy, and darken our outlook. As I grow in my faith, I find the circumstances of life have less of an effect on me. I am able to pull myself up and out of whatever is going on and focus on Him, trusting fully in Him and His ability to make all things new.

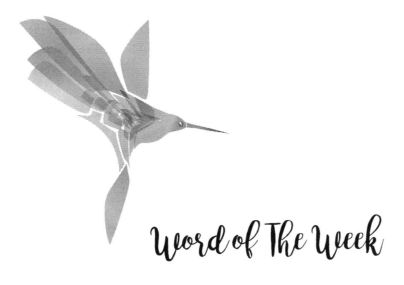

Word of The Week

GLADNESS

Gladness is a feeling or state of well-being and contentment. The feeling of contentment is so fulfilling. It brings about the feelings of peace, satisfaction, and a sense of positivity. The smile you have on your face after you nail a difficult presentation at work or when you see an "A" on a paper you've worked long and hard on is contagious. Pick one person this week to share your love of God with so that they may also experience this sense of gladness.

Shall we Pray?

Lord help us to be excited this week! Excited and exulted about all you are doing in and through us. Help us to spread kindness and joy like confetti. We know that a smile and even laughter can be contagious. Uplifting others is a gift in itself and helping them to come to know you an even better gift. Our relationship with you bring us a sense of contentment and peace that is difficult to explain. It's like having the best kept secret but one that we want to share. Let us help other's experience this precious joy that we hold in our hearts. We ask that you use us in whatever way possible to be the hands and feet of God. We ask these and other blessings in your name this day – amen

listen to your heart

- I feel: _____
- I need: _____
- I forgive: _____
- I celebrate: _____
- I release: _____
- I trust: _____

The best thing about this week was

_____

_____

Me time — self care commitment

_____

_____

I was grateful for:

_____

_____

_____

_____

_____

_____

It's time to
daydream

_____

_____

_____

_____

_____

_____

_____

_____

_____

_____

_____

_____

_____

_____

Let your Mind Soar

Week twenty-three:
May you be strengthened with all power, according to his glorious might, for all endurance and patience with joy

COLOSSIANS 1:11 (RSV)

I love the power instilled in this verse. I always say God is my superpower and this verse really speaks to how He truly is our power source. All we have to do is tap into it—it is there, waiting for us. I challenge you to let the power of the Lord's words resonate within you and give you the strength and endurance you need this week.

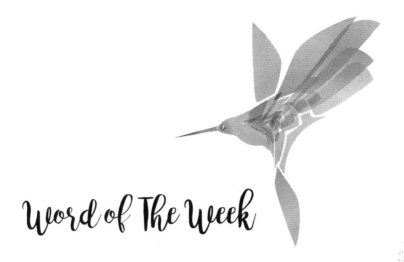

Word of The Week

ENDURANCE

The power to endure an unpleasant or difficult process or situation without giving way is endurance. Just like an athlete builds endurance through daily training, we gain endurance in our faith journey by studying the Word of God. In my weakest moments and during my toughest times, it was my faith that pulled me up and out. Burying myself in the Word strengthened me and gave me just what I needed to push through. Is there something that has been dragging you down or something that you need to work through? Repeat this scripture every morning this week to help build your endurance and stamina in the Lord.

Shall we Pray?

My God, my God – life can indeed be so difficult and so tedious at times. We go from the highest of highs to the lowest of lows and many days find it difficult to put one foot in front of the other. As Christians we are not immune to trouble. Just because we have a strong faith does not mean we tough times don't come our way. The hope and prayer however, is that we stay grounded in your word and that we persevere and push through putting all of our faith in you. When we have this innate trust it gives us a unique confidence and outlook on life and we can face each trial and tribulation with unwavering strength. No we are not always happy but we know who is on the throne and we trust that you've got us. I ask that you please cover everyone this week and give them the resolve and endurance they need to make it through. Place the word deep in their heart and let them reflect on it when necessary. Be our guide and our strength today and always. Amen.

Listen to your heart

- I feel: _____
- I need: _____
- I forgive: _____
- I celebrate: _____
- I release: _____
- I trust: _____

The best thing about this week was

_____

_____

Me time—self care commitment

_____

_____

_____

I was grateful for:

_____

_____

_____

_____

_____

_____

Set Your Mind Free

Just Imagine

Week twenty-four:
But now I am coming to you, and these things I speak in the world, that they may have my joy fulfilled in themselves.

– JOHN 17:13 (ESV)

This scripture reminds me that there is power in our words. I have always been enamored by the written word. I love to journal, write letters, and send cards. There is just a significance to me in words. Their meaning has great power and the ability to influence others in positive or negative ways. There is no greater role model than God—throughout the Bible, He teaches us the power of our words and how to use them effectively. Speak truth, speak abundance, speak love and peace—speak life!

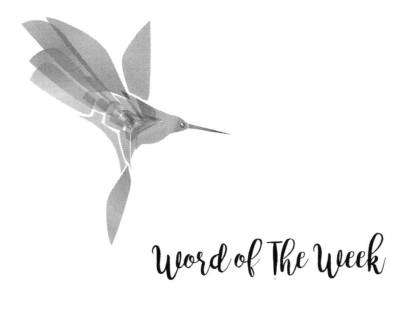

Word of The Week

POWER

The capacity or ability to direct or influence the behavior of others. Can you commit this week to limiting the negative words we sometimes so easily speak? Start your day with a positive affirmation vs. feelings of defeat or negativity.

Shall we Pray?

Lord we come to you today seeking your power and your knowledge. You have told us that the tongue has the power of life and death. Our words can speak life or speak death and we can build others up or tear them down just by opening our mouths to speak without stopping to think first. Help us Lord to recognize the power of a pause. Thinking before we speak or respond could save each of us so much turmoil and heartache. Prepare our hearts and minds this week to focus on speaking life and spreading the love and light of God. We do all things to glorify you and we give you thanks and praise today and always. Amen.

listen to your heart

- I feel: _____

- I need: _____

- I forgive: _____

- I celebrate: _____

- I release: _____

- I trust: _____

The best thing about this week was

_____

_____

Me time—self care commitment

_____

_____

I was grateful for:

_____

_____

_____

_____

_____

_____

It's time to daydream

_____

_____

_____

_____

_____

_____

_____

_____

_____

_____

_____

_____

_____

_____

_____

Let your Mind Soar

Week twenty-five:
So that by God's will I may come to you with joy and be refreshed in your company.

– ROMANS 15:32 (ESV)

Sometimes we need to be refreshed; we need a pick-me-up. Going to the Lord in prayer can give you just the boost you need. Spending a little time with Him puts everything in perspective! My co-workers can tell you first hand that there are many a day that I have to take a time-out. I may get a little quiet at my desk while I spend a few minutes in prayer, or I may excuse myself for a quick walk so I can have a little talk with Jesus. I used to limit these times in my day, feeling like I had to stay focused on work or that there wasn't time. But I know this is not the answer for me. I will be more productive and in a better state of mind when I take my moments with Him. It can even be as simple as plugging into one of my favorite inspirational songs or reading a memorable devotional. Whatever the choice, His word refreshes me and keeps me focused on leading in love.

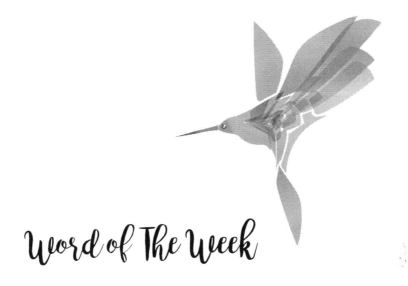

Word of The Week

REFRESH

To refresh is to give new strength or energy to; reinvigorate. God gives us fresh, anointing and fresh grace each and every day. When we open our eyes each morning, it is indeed a blessing, and we should approach each day feeling the refreshening of God. Focus on have a refreshed perspective this week. Our perspective easily becomes our reality. What negative perspective in your life needs refreshed?

Shall we Pray?

Heavenly Father, we come to you asking you to give us a renewed perspective and a refreshed outlook as we begin a new week. When we begin to feel bogged down or stressed help us to come to you to be lifted and encouraged. Allow us to speak to ourselves lovingly and to not be so hard on ourselves. We must learn to be gentle with ourselves and to give ourselves grace when we need it. Melt away our hardened hearts and help us to lead with love this week. Let us show empathy and compassion to others and when we are faced with a challenge instead of us filling our minds with negative rhetoric let us speak a positive word of encouragement. We bless your holy name and thank you for all that you do – amen.

Listen to your heart

- I feel: _____
- I need: _____
- I forgive: _____
- I celebrate: _____
- I release: _____
- I trust: _____

The best thing about this week was

_____

_____

Me time – self care commitment

_____

_____

_____

I was grateful for:

_____

_____

_____

_____

_____

_____

Set Your Mind Free

Just Imagine

Week twenty-six:

The LORD your God is in your midst, a mighty one who will save; he will rejoice over you with gladness; he will quiet you by his love; he will exult over you with loud singing.

– ZEPHANIAH 3:17 (ESV)

I love this verse. It reminds us that God has our back in all things. He is there for us in good times and in bad. To lift us up when we are down and cheer us on when we need support. Quite frankly, He is our everything! In my darkest moments, when I felt the most alone and like no one could possibly understand what I was going through, I relied on my faith. There are times in our lives when no one can help or can fix it. The only one we can rely on for strength and direction is the Lord. It can feel lonely, but day by day, He will show you He is there, working it all out behind the scenes. His ways are not our ways, and He has proven it to me over and over again. From miscarriages, to divorce, to betrayals from those I loved and trusted, God remains the same yesterday, today, and tomorrow.

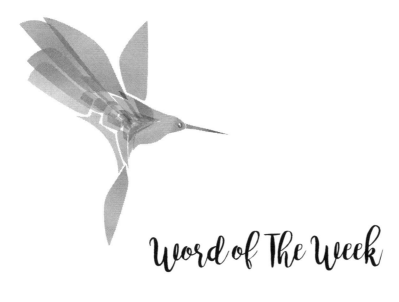

Word of The Week

SOURCE

A source is a place, person, or thing from which something comes from or can be obtained. God is our ultimate source. He remains unchanging and always has our best interest at heart. This week, when you are feeling alone, tap into your "source" and let Him take over!

Shall we Pray?

Lord you are our rock. Our power and the ultimate source. No weapon formed against us shall prosper. We place it all in your hands and walk with power into this week. We ask that you go before us and that you keep us from all hurt, harm and danger. When doubt enters our minds or we are about to falter, help us to remain steadfast and resilient and to stand firmly on your word. You've got us all in the palm of your hands and will lead and guide us through it all. We remain in awe of you, your will and your enduring love for us. Amen.

listen to your heart

- I feel: _____
- I need: _____
- I forgive: _____
- I celebrate: _____
- I release: _____
- I trust: _____

The best thing about this week was

_____

_____

Me time—self care commitment

_____

_____

I was grateful for:

_____

_____

_____

_____

_____

_____

It's time to daydream

_____

_____

_____

_____

_____

_____

_____

_____

_____

_____

_____

_____

_____

Let your Mind Soar

Week twenty-seven:
Your words were found, and I ate them, and your words became to me a joy and the delight of my heart, for I am called by your name, O LORD, God of hosts

– JEREMIAH 15:16 (ESV)

If we study the Word and keep our minds and hearts focused on Him, He will fill our lives with unspeakable joy. These words will be etched in our hearts and minds and become a part of who we are. I have always struggled with memorizing Scripture. As a child, I would learn it for Sunday School or for class, and then it was gone. I became obsessed with wanting to be one of those people who can just recite Scripture. I bought a new Study Bible and read it daily. I indulged in Bible plans on my Bible app—everything I could think of to become a student of the Word. What I realized is that my life experiences are what have taught me the most about scriptures. It took me living, making mistakes, failing, having successes, heartbreaks, and wins to truly embrace and understand those scriptures I spent so much time studying. The Word truly became a part of me, and I can speak to it freely. I still wish I could recite them all verbatim, but I'll get there as I keep on living!

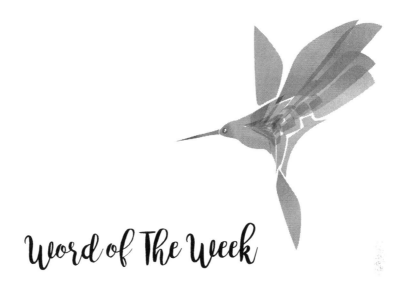

Word of The Week

BLUEPRINT

A blueprint is a design plan or model. Allow the Word of God to be your blueprint. We rely daily on our GPS in our phones or our cars and believe that they will lead us to our destination. Why wouldn't we put this same trust in our Father? He has proven to us time and time again to be reliable, on time, and accurate. Focus on this verse this week whenever you are feeling at a loss for direction or answers.

Shall we Pray?

Lord, let your word be our compass. Let it guide our thoughts and our actions and lead us in the right direction. It is all really so much more simple than we make it. You are the way, the truth and the light. If we stay focused on you nothing else matters around us. Be with us this week and catch us when we fall. Help us to seek you first when we do know or cannot find the answers. Let our pride go by the wayside and allow us to be vulnerable and open to the direction you have for our lives. Your plans are greater than anything we could ever imagine. We ask this prayer and other blessings in your mighty, matchless name. Amen

Listen to your heart

- I feel: _____
- I need: _____
- I forgive: _____
- I celebrate: _____
- I release: _____
- I trust: _____

The best thing about this week was

_____
_____

Me time – self care commitment

_____
_____
_____

I was grateful for:

_____
_____
_____
_____
_____
_____

Set Your
Mind Free

Just Imagine

Week twenty-eight:
You have made known to me the paths of life; you will make me full of gladness with your presence

– ACTS 2:28 (ESV)

God gives us the blueprint to living a life full of love, grace, and fulfillment. All we have to do is let Him in, and He will lead the way! Are you a planner? Do you think your plans are the only way to go? I have to admit that I am a planner. I always have a to-do list and a back-up plan or two. However, God has shown me my shortfalls and probably has gotten so many laughs watching me think I was in charge. What I have learned is that when I stick to His plan and am obedient to His direction in my life, my life flows so much easier. We make it so much harder than it has to be. Let go of the reigns and let God.

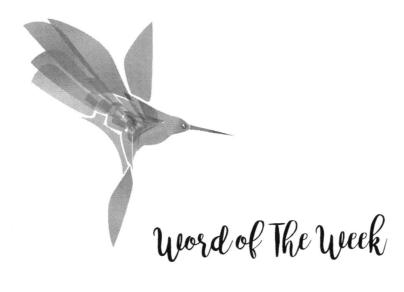

Word of The Week

GUIDE

A person who advises or shows the way to others is a guide. Instead of allowing our alarms, cell phones, and GPS to guide our lives this week, rely on God. I love technology, but it is a blessing and a curse. We place way too much value in it as opposed to our relationships with the people in our lives, let alone our God. What aspect of your life will you trust God with this week?

Shall we Pray?

Heavenly Father we seek your help this week. We know we are guilty of believing that we are in charge of what happens in our lives. Time and time again you show us in your way that it is you who is in control. Your reign on the throne and your power is mighty.

Please takeover our lives and show us that your will be done is the way in which we should live. The sooner we stop trying to control our outcomes the better off we will be. Give us a clean heart and allow us to see ourselves clearly and to work on our shortfalls.

With you leading our lives we know we shall not fail. We give you all the praise and all the glory, amen.

listen to your heart

- I feel: _____
- I need: _____
- I forgive: _____
- I celebrate: _____
- I release: _____
- I trust: _____

The best thing about this week was

_____

_____

Me time – self care commitment

_____

_____

I was grateful for:

_____

_____

_____

_____

_____

_____

It's time to daydream

Let your
Mind Soar

Week twenty-nine:
His master said to him, 'Well done, good and faithful servant. You have been faithful over a little; I will set you over much. Enter into the joy of your master.

MATTHEW 25:21 (ESV)

I believe many times God is testing us along our journey. The trouble or difficult times in life are many times lessons for us to grow and do and be better. When we show Him that we can handle the smaller things, He adds to our plate and enlarges our territory. It's all about how we handle the test! Sometimes we have to re-take it when the lesson has not been learned. Pay attention—He is always speaking to us! I can attest to this scripture showing up in my life. I can also say that sometimes our tests are not even for or about us. Sometimes the lessons we go through are for others so that they don't repeat our mistakes. That is the beauty of God working in our lives. Our obedience will always be rewarded.

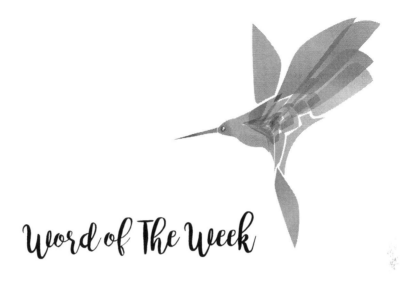

Word of The Week

TEST

Testing is a procedure intended to establish the quality, performance, or reliability of something. Life itself is a test, but we don't approach it the way we did our exams in school. We just go along living, not realizing life is full of lessons God needs us to master. There is purpose in our pain and in the failures we have had. What test do you feel you have to keep retaking in life? Study the details to see where you are going wrong and repeating past behaviors. God has all the answers.

Shall we Pray?

You are the alpha and the omega – you are so worthy to be praised. We lift you name and are careful to give you all the honor and all the glory. Time and time again we repeat our mistakes and are remiss in learning the lesson you have so clearly sent to us. We ignore the quiet whisper of your voice and power through life on our own terms. Lord we ask that this stops today. Give us the courage to accept the things we cannot change and eyes to see things for what they truly are. Help us to slow down for a moment to truly glean the messages you give us so clearly each day. We want to be the best version of ourselves and we know that you are working so hard to get us there. Help us get out of our own way. We love you Lord and thank you in advance for all you are doing in our lives. Amen.

Listen to your heart

- I feel: _____
- I need: _____
- I forgive: _____
- I celebrate: _____
- I release: _____
- I trust: _____

The best thing about this week was

_____
_____

Me time - self care commitment

_____
_____
_____

I was grateful for:

_____
_____
_____
_____
_____
_____

Set Your Mind Free

Just Imagine

Week thirty:
Just so, I tell you, there will be more joy in heaven over one sinner who repents than over ninety-nine righteous persons who need no repentance.

– LUKE 15:7 (ESV)

There is such joy in the gift of salvation and learning someone has given their life to Christ. The angels truly rejoice and so should we! I don't think we realize the significance of someone giving their life to Christ. I remember doing so myself, but I was a young child. What I knew for sure was that I didn't want to go to hell. I was too young to fully understand what salvation meant and the important role it would play in my life. I want to experience the fullness of the gift of salvation that Jesus died to give us. In order to do so, I must remain consistent, never give up, never give in, and stand strong on everything salvation has afforded me.

Word of The Week

SALVATION

The deliverance from sin and it's circumstances. Are you familiar with the prayer of salvation? It is a simple prayer that you may have prayed in church or in your readings. *"Dear Lord Jesus, I know that I am a sinner, and I ask for your forgiveness. I believe You died for my sins and rose from the dead. I turn from my sins and invite You to come into my heart and life. I want to trust and follow you as my Lord and Savior."* If you need to pray this prayer for yourself, please do so. Is there someone on your heart that you feel led to share the gift of salvation with? If so, don't be afraid to act on your instincts—your obedience will be rewarded.

Shall we Pray?

Holy, holy, holy – Lord God our Father, we thank you for your love and your sacrifice. We don't take for granted that you didn't have to give your only begotten son for our future. You love us just that much. Let us allow the magnitude of your gift to permeate our hearts and our minds. Help us Lord to lead others to your kingdom. We know that the angles rejoice each and every time one of your children accepts you as their Lord and Savior. Let us lead a life of peace, love, kindness and acceptance of others. Help us not to pass judgement on our neighbor but to open our hearts lovingly to them. If we have the opportunity this week to spread the good news please don't let us be afraid but to be confident in what we stand for. We are your soldiers and have work to do. Be with us always Lord. We love you and we praise your mighty name – amen.

listen to your heart

- I feel: _____
- I need: _____
- I forgive: _____
- I celebrate: _____
- I release: _____
- I trust: _____

The best thing about this week was

_____

_____

Me time – self care commitment

_____

_____

I was grateful for:

_____

_____

_____

_____

_____

_____

It's time to daydream

Let your Mind Soar

Week thirty-one:

I have said these things to you, that in me you may have peace. In the world you will have tribulation. But take heart; I have overcome the world.

JOHN 16:33 (ESV)

Life can be difficult. In fact, it is sometimes downright debilitating. But we can take heart in the fact that God is always there for us. He has taken one for the team so to speak and can handle any one of our issues with ease! There is nothing too hard for our God! I am a witness to this. He has shown me so many times that when I am weak He is strong. During my pregnancy, I was told early on that the doctors were cautiously optimistic that I would be able to carry my daughter. During my weekly visits and ultrasounds, they measured and analyzed my pregnancy to see if she was growing and progressing as needed. The doctors, nurses, and tests left me each week on pins and needles. They'd tell me things looked "okay," and that we'd see where we were the following week. Your pregnancy is supposed to be a happy time—or so I thought. Mine was stressful, and even as I passed the critical twentieth week, I was still told it was unlikely I'd carry to full term, and that we would need to plan to get to week 32. I had a choice. I could either live in fear or trust that God had this, and that He—not the doctors—was in control. I chose the latter and begin to be happy about the beautiful life growing inside me. I made it to twenty-eight (and a half) weeks, but the key is we made it! Fourteen years later, I look at my miracle baby and know God remains on the throne.

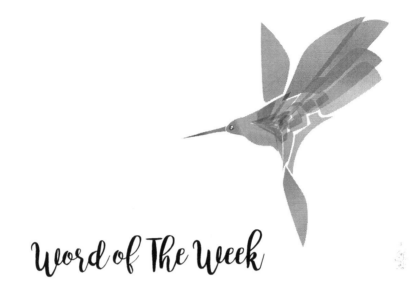

Word of The Week

TRIALS

Trials are a test of the performance, qualities, or suitability of someone or something. Think back on a trial you had to endure and the strength or wisdom gained from it. Trials have a way of making us appreciate our growth. There is always purpose in our pain. What trials in your life have resulted in the most personal growth?

Shall we Pray?

Most gracious Father, I ask that you strengthen and sustain each person reading this prayer through the trials they may be facing this week. So much of the time we feel our weaknesses are being exposed during our trying times when in reality it is our strengths that are being made clear. Help us to understand that there is a lesson in everything and a missing piece of the puzzle that we need to move forward on our journey. You are equipping us with what we need. We will look back on these times and recognize your hand in it all. Pruning us just like a farmer or gardener does with their crops and flowers.

We will bloom beautifully as there is always a little rain before the rainbow. Wrap your loving arms around us Lord and remind us that we are never alone. We give you all the glory and pray in your mighty and majestic name. Amen

Listen to your heart

- I feel: _____
- I need: _____
- I forgive: _____
- I celebrate: _____
- I release: _____
- I trust: _____

The best thing about this week was

_____

_____

Me time – self care commitment

_____

_____

_____

I was grateful for:

_____

_____

_____

_____

_____

_____

Set Your Mind Free

Just Imagine

Week thirty-two:
For the sake of Christ, then, I am content with weaknesses, insults, hardships, persecutions, and calamities. For when I am weak, then I am strong.

- 2 CORINTHIANS 12:10 (ESV)

In God's eyes, we are true perfection. His masterpieces. What anyone else thinks or says is irrelevant. Don't allow others' opinions to affect you in any way; continue to walk in excellence! Self-acceptance has been a life-long struggle for me, and I am sure I am not alone. As women, we tend to hold ourselves to a higher standard. We seek to be perfect mothers, wives, partners, professionals, friends, and more. When I finally acknowledged that I was accepted as is in God's sight, I began to worry less about how others felt about me. I became unapologetic and embraced all of me. God makes no mistakes.

Word of The Week

ACCEPTANCE

Acceptance is the action or process of being received as adequate or suitable. What are some things or qualities you struggle to accept about yourself? Choose one quality and focus this week on embracing that element of yourself. We are all perfectly imperfect.

Shall we Pray?

Heavenly Father, please hear our cry. We need you, every day we need you. Help us to seek you first in all things. When we focus on you the importance of other people and things lessens. There is so much noise in the world and it is so easy to get caught up in all of the comparisons that so naturally happen. We ask that you be with us this week as we focus on embracing all of who we are and who you made us to be. When we question who we are we are in actuality questioning you. You make no mistakes and as Psalm 139 reminds us we are fearfully and wonderfully made. Help us to live authentically and to walk confidently in you. Amen

listen to your heart

- I feel: _____
- I need: _____
- I forgive: _____
- I celebrate: _____
- I release: _____
- I trust: _____

The best thing about this week was

_____
_____

Me time—self care commitment

_____
_____

I was grateful for:

_____
_____
_____
_____
_____
_____

It's time to daydream

_____

_____

_____

_____

_____

_____

_____

_____

_____

_____

_____

_____

_____

_____

_____

Let your Mind Soar

Week thirty-three:
For David said about him, I saw the Lord before me at all times; he is near me, and I will not be troubled.

– ACTS 2:25 (GNT)

God's presence is always near; He is with us at all times, even those days we feel alone and that no one cares. He cares about every hair on our heads! His loves surrounds us like a huge, warm hug! I find myself looking for "God winks" throughout my day and week. Those moments when God reminds us He is with us. It can be the surprise of seeing a rainbow while out running errands, the beauty of blooming flowers or trees, the random text you receive from a loved one telling you are in your thoughts, or an unexpected card in the mail just saying "hello." One of my daily practices is listing three great things that have happened in my day. These three things can range from big event-driven situations like receiving an unexpected gift or flowers to taking a nap or seeing my favorite hummingbirds stop by for a visit. In all of it, I find God's voice reminding me of His love for me.

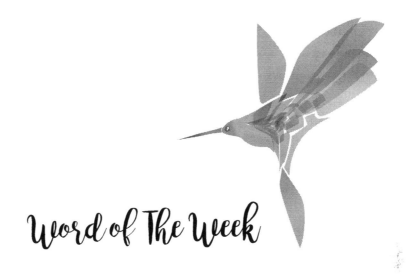

Word of The Week

PRESENCE

A person or a thing that exists or is present in a place but is not seen. God's presence is all around us; we only have to open our hearts to see it. When do you feel God's presence the most? Is it in the mornings during a quiet time? When you take a walk or are in a specific place? I feel His presence in the changing colors of the sky during sunrise or sunset, watching the breeze sway the leaves of the trees, listening to the ocean, and watching children play. Dedicate a time each day to focus on how God shows up in your life

Shall we Pray?

Dearest Father – we come to you today as humbly as we know how, thanking you in advance for all you have done and will do in our lives. Help us to notice your amazing presence in our lives. We are often times so busy that we don't notice the beauty and God winks all around us. Help us to slow down and open our eyes to all of your gifts. We all have a God voice and must learn to recognize and react to it. Please help make it clear to us so that we have this tool to help us through our days. We can never thank you enough and we give you all the praise, honor and glory, in Jesus' name amen.

Listen to your heart

- I feel: _____
- I need: _____
- I forgive: _____
- I celebrate: _____
- I release: _____
- I trust: _____

The best thing about this week was

_____
_____

Me time – self care commitment

_____
_____
_____

I was grateful for:

_____
_____
_____
_____
_____
_____

Set Your Mind Free

Just Imagine

Week thirty-four:
May all who seek you rejoice and be glad in you; may those who love your saving help always say, The LORD is great!

– PSALM 70:4 (NIV)

My hope every day is that others see the light and love of God in something I do—in my words or actions. You don't have to walk around with your Bible in hand to spread the love of Christ. I have learned during these past few months how much the saying "the church is more than four walls" means. Because of this pandemic, we've not been able to worship as we traditionally do in the building of the church, and we've been forced to listen to our sermons online. But I have been stretched by this experience, and find myself spending more time with my Bible study group exploring the words and sharing life lessons. I have reached out to those in my life struggling during these unprecedented times to pray with them, and have even participated in an online daily prayer group, praying live on Facebook. If you'd have asked me a year ago if I'd be doing these things to spread His Word and build the kingdom, I'd say "no way!" But it is happening, and I love the personal growth I have experienced.

Word of The Week

REJOICE

To rejoice is to feel or show great joy or delight. We have no problem showing our delight or joy when watching our favorite sports teams kick a field goal or score a three-pointer in overtime. Why do we become shy with sharing our love of God? How can you show your love and excitement for God this week?

Shall we Pray?

Our most gracious God we love and exalt your holy name. Help us not to shy away from our love for you and to proudly share your word with those we come in contact with. We never know who is watching and listening to us. For many we are the only God they see or Bible they read. It is our actions father and our treatment of others that makes the biggest statement. How do we treat those around us? Do we offer help to those in need? With businesses and places of worship closed or with limited access, we have to find other ways to spread the word of Christ. We must be creative and continue to rejoice over our king. Guide us Lord and help us do the work that is necessary to build your kingdom. We love and adore you, amen.

listen to your heart

- I feel: _____
- I need: _____
- I forgive: _____
- I celebrate: _____
- I release: _____
- I trust: _____

The best thing about this week was

_____

_____

Me time—self care commitment

_____

_____

I was grateful for:

_____

_____

_____

_____

_____

It's time to daydream

Let your Mind Soar

Week thirty-five:

Now to him who is able to keep you from stumbling and to present you blameless before the presence of his glory with great joy.

– JUDE 1:24 (ESV)

God has us all in the palm of His hand. What reassurance that gives me on a daily basis! He's our protector, He will fight for us, and He continues to forgive us and love us in spite of ourselves! I think we forget sometimes that we are God's children. He does not ever want to see us hurting, sad, or broken. In the same way we protect our children or the loved ones in our lives, He wants to protect us. It makes me think of my daughter when she was young and had a "boo boo" or was at the doctor about to get a shot. She would look at me, and with trusting eyes, ask me if it was going to hurt. My response to her then and even now is "Would mommy ever do anything to hurt you? Do you trust mommy?" This is the same way God wants us to look towards Him. Understanding that even when it hurts, His goal is to protect us, to love us, and to help us make it all better. We will stumble, we will have falls and boo-boos, but He always has our backs.

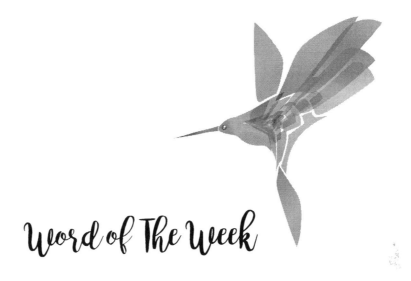

Word of The Week

PROTECTOR

A protector is someone or something who keeps anything from happening to someone or something. When I first see or hear the word "protector," I think of a mama bear and her bear cub, a lion and his young, or a father looking out for his family. God encompasses all of this and seeks to cover us every day to heal us from all hurt, harm, and danger. How has God shown you that is he is guiding and protecting you lately?

Shall we Pray?

Lord, our protector, strong tower and shield, we lay down our burdens at your feet. You go before us and make our crooked paths straight. As we begin a new week, we carry this truth with us and are reassured. Placing our trust in you allows us to exhale and proceed on our life's journey without fear or worry. We take dominion over every place we step foot because we know who our Father is. Help us to cling to this unyielding love whenever we have doubts or anxious moments. You are good and greatly to be praised. Amen.

Listen to your heart

- I feel: _____
- I need: _____
- I forgive: _____
- I celebrate: _____
- I release: _____
- I trust: _____

The best thing about this week was

_____

_____

Me time – self care commitment

_____

_____

I was grateful for:

_____

_____

_____

_____

_____

_____

Set Your Mind Free

Just Imagine

Week thirty-six:
Serve the Lord with gladness! Come into his presence with singing!

- PSALM 100:2 (ESV)

Anything that we do in God's name should be done with joy and gladness in our hearts. As children of God, we must realize that people are watching us—my goal every day is to be sure others see His love and goodness in me, through my actions, words, and deeds. I have to say you just never know who is watching your example. I shared an article on the LinkedIn platform regarding racial inequality and how, as leaders and managers in corporate America, it is important to address how our employees are handling the stresses brought on by not only COVID-19 but by the social unrest. An old boss of mine did not like my sharing of this topic on what he deemed a professional network that should only be used for job information and networking. I did not respond on the public post, but sent him a personal note respectfully explaining my position, although he had not given me the same respect. I thanked him for his opinion and moved on, taking the high road. Well, not only did he respond back defending his views, but he went back and forth with me. I finally said "Let's agree to disagree," and was very disappointed and disheartened by the exchange. He is a leader in his organization and if this is his thinking, how will his employees feel? Not my problem, though, so again—I moved on. Well, what I didn't know was that he was receiving a tremendous amount of negative feedback from his response to my post. He was called out by friends and colleagues. He came back to me over a week later with an apology and shared that his eyes had indeed been opened. I could have responded to him in anger, but God did the dirty work for me and in the end, more of His love was shared with others through perspective!

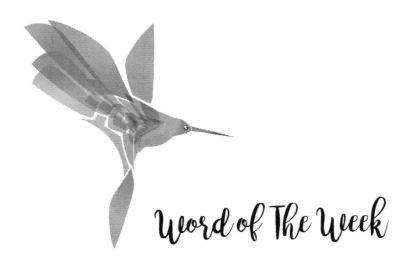

Word of The Week

REPRESENT

Representing is to be entitled or appointed to act or speak for someone or something. As children of God, it is up to us to represent Him at all times, not just when it's easy or feels good. We are to build His kingdom, and that means taking the high road many days when we want to just stay low. Pausing before you respond to a comment, e-mail, or conversation can sometimes be all it takes for us to respond in love. What kind of representation are you going to show this week as a child of God?

Shall we Pray?

Our most gracious Father, your word tells us to "Do all things in love". This is not always easy Lord, but we ask for your help. Help us to see the good in people before the bad. To have empathy for those around us and not to condemn others before we've walked in their shoes. We are all going through something and have a story to tell. The sooner we realize this the sooner we can work together to do your will. You ask us to love one another as you love us. It such a simple ask Lord and we make it hard. We ask that you touch our hearts and that we lead with them instead of our minds. Give us a heart of compassion, empathy, understanding and grace. We ask these and other blessings in your name this day – amen.

listen to your heart

- I feel: _____
- I need: _____
- I forgive: _____
- I celebrate: _____
- I release: _____
- I trust: _____

The best thing about this week was

_____

_____

Me time—self care commitment

_____

_____

I was grateful for:

_____

_____

_____

_____

_____

_____

It's time to daydream

_____

_____

_____

_____

_____

_____

_____

_____

_____

_____

_____

_____

_____

_____

Let your Mind Soar

Week thirty-seven:
I have no greater joy than to hear that my children are walking in the truth.

- JOHN 1:4 (ESV)

As a mom, nothing brings me greater joy than to hear my daughter reciting the Word, hearing her pray, or referencing God's presence in her life. Watching her on her faith journey is the biggest blessing! I realize as a parent that we want to give our kids the best of everything, but one of the best gifts I can bestow upon my child is helping her build her faith muscle, teaching her the Word, and exemplifying grace. Our children watch us and emulate everything we do. Their values are formed by the experiences we give them. I love the holidays and to entertain, and I watch how my daughter plans fun activities with her friends, inviting them over for Friendsgiving or creating fun videos to celebrate their birthdays. She's gaining these values and love of hospitality from home. While this makes my heart happy, there is no greater joy as a mom than knowing she knows and trusts the Lord.

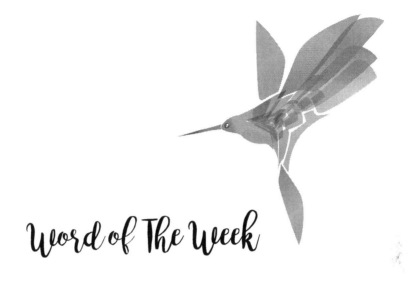

Word of The Week

BLESSINGS

Blessings are God's favor and protection. There is a huge difference between being lucky and being blessed. I am always clear that the positive things happening in my life are not due to luck but God's grace. I am blessed. Luck is based on chance—our God is the real deal. If you had to share the biggest blessings in your life, what would they be?

Shall we Pray?

Heavenly Father, we could never thank you enough for the way you bless and cover us. Blessings seen and unseen, you grace us with your goodness every day. Help us Lord to never take you for granted. Help us to recognize the favor you have shown us on so many occasions. We are so humbled by your love for us and want nothing more than to please you. Be with us this week and show us ways we can be a blessing to others. Ways in which we can spread you love and light. We are forever grateful and give you all the praise, all the honor and all the glory. Amen

Listen to your heart

- I feel: _____
- I need: _____
- I forgive: _____
- I celebrate: _____
- I release: _____
- I trust: _____

The best thing about this week was

_____

_____

Me time—self care commitment

_____

_____

_____

I was grateful for:

_____

_____

_____

_____

_____

_____

Set Your Mind Free

Just
Imagine

Week thirty-eight:
Let everything that has breath praise the LORD! Praise the LORD!

- PSALM 150:6 (ESV)

When we praise God, we are showing our love and adoration of Him! Nothing makes Him happier than when we lift our voices to Him. When I wake up in the morning and hear the birds chirping, I imagine they are sharing their praise too, or even when the wind is moving, through the leaves and branches of the trees. They too are showing their love of our omnipotent Lord as they sway and move. I have two hummingbirds that come and visit daily. I don't have a feeder or anything in particular to draw them to my home. I believe they are my angels that watch over me daily. I love watching them swoop in and out and chase after each other. It's as if they are dancing with each other and just having the best time. The joy they bring me makes me think it is how they show their praise. Whether it is through song, dance, or prayer, we were created to praise Him! Nothing gives Him more satisfaction than us lifting and praising His name.

Word of The Week

ADORATION

Adoring something is to demonstrate deep love and respect. There is only 1 God for me – only one being I worship. Adoration encompasses respect, reverence, and devotion. His name will continually be in my mouth and in all my ways I will acknowledge Him. How do you show God and others your love and gratitude?

Shall we Pray?

Lord, we ask that you touch us and give us a spirit of praise as we go into this week. Help us to lift our voices and magnify our love for you. Whether it be in song, dance or whatever medium we choose, let us lift your name on high. You are so deserving of our praise and it should be a part of our every day life. We love to sing your praises and are so thankful for you in our lives. You are worthy to be praised today and always. Amen

listen to your heart

- I feel: _____
- I need: _____
- I forgive: _____
- I celebrate: _____
- I release: _____
- I trust: _____

The best thing about
this week was

_____
_____

Me time – self care
commitment

_____
_____

I was grateful
for:

_____
_____
_____
_____
_____
_____

It's time to daydream

_____

_____

_____

_____

_____

_____

_____

_____

_____

_____

_____

_____

_____

_____

Let your
Mind Soar

Week thirty-nine:
A glad heart makes a cheerful face, but by sorrow of heart the spirit is crushed.

- PROVERBS 15:13 (ESV)

True joy starts on the inside! When you are at peace and have joy in your heart, it emanates from the inside out. Happiness is based on what is happening around us while joy is based on what is happening within us! Our joy comes from above, and the true gift is that no matter what you are dealing with, when you have joy in your heart, it gives you the wherewithal to power through. I have had people ask me during some trying times in my life how I can keep smiling. How do I still have joy, but the answer is easy for me. God gave me this joy, and the world cannot take it away. The secret to joy is seeking God where we doubt He is—in the rough times, in the disappointments, and even in the heartbreak. God is always with us.

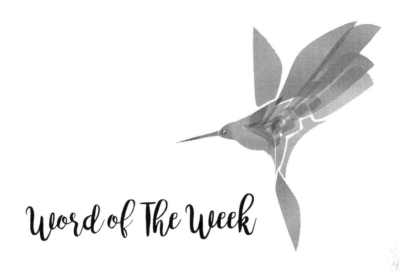

Word of The Week

JOYOUS

Joyousness is being full of happiness and joy in connection with events, things, times, and places. What are some of the small things that bring you the greatest joy? It can be the simplest of things for me—finding time to meditate, a hot cup of peppermint tea, or buying fresh flowers. Think of those little things that make your heart happy. Try to be sure you include one or a few of them in your days this week.

Shall we Pray?

Our dearest heavenly Father, I ask that you please touch each and every heart reading this prayer. Help them to understand the true meaning of joy and how very different it is from happiness. Joy is truly a choice and it is grounded in our faith. It is not based on a situation or circumstance. It is not fleeting, here one moment and gone the next. True joy is in our hearts and rooted in our gratitude. Be with each and everyone of us and keep our focus on those things that make our hearts happy. Let us be reminded that it truly is the little things that bring us the most joy. Help us to stay grounded in our faith and live life to it's fullest each and every day. We thank you in advance for your mercies. Amen.

Listen to your heart

- I feel: _____
- I need: _____
- I forgive: _____
- I celebrate: _____
- I release: _____
- I trust: _____

The best thing about this week was

_____
_____

Me time - self care commitment

_____
_____
_____

I was grateful for:

_____
_____
_____
_____
_____
_____

Set Your Mind Free

Just Imagine

Week forty:

One thing I ask from the LORD, this only do I seek: that I may dwell in the house of the LORD all the days of my life, to gaze on the beauty of the LORD and to seek him in his temple.

- PSALM 27:4 (NIV)

While I love the feeling I have anytime I enter the house of the Lord, I have come to realize that the "church" is so much more than the four walls of the building. We are the church, the hands of feet of God. It is up to us to represent His love and spread the good news wherever we are! 2020 has truly taught me the importance of this. With so much sadness and despair, people are seeking solace and peace. The building itself has not been able to be open, and through the beauty of technology, we have been able to bring the church into our homes. Sunday services, Bible studies, small groups, and online classes have helped to fill the void. Prayer groups have popped up on Facebook, Zoom calls, and even neighbors have joined together to have their own worship services. While I do miss the hugs and communion I share with the members of my church, my heart and spirit are still being fed.

Word of The Week

CHURCH

A building used for public Christian worship is called a "church." What does the church signify to you? How has it impacted your life in a positive or even a negative way?

Shall we Pray?

Dear God we come to you giving you thanks for all you do for us each and every day. These are trying and heavy times and we have been forced to dig deep to find solace from the world and it's ugliness. We ask that you show us ways to keep our spirit fed. We must strive to stay in your word for we can be so easily swayed by all of the confusion around us. You are the way, the truth and the light and we are so grateful for your unending love for us. Lift us and guide and keep us on solid ground. We are soldiers in your army and are committed to living life according to your word. We pray these and other blessings in your name this day. Amen.

listen to your heart

- I feel: _____
- I need: _____
- I forgive: _____
- I celebrate: _____
- I release: _____
- I trust: _____

The best thing about this week was

_____

_____

Me time—self care commitment

_____

_____

I was grateful for:

_____

_____

_____

_____

_____

_____

It's time to daydream

Let your Mind Soar

Week forty-one:

Do you not know? Have you not heard? The LORD is the everlasting God, the Creator of the ends of the earth. He will not grow tired or weary, and his understanding no one can fathom. He gives strength to the weary and increases the power of the weak. Even youths grow tired and weary, and young men stumble and fall; but those who hope in the LORD will renew their strength. They will soar on wings like eagles; they will run and not grow weary, they will walk and not be faint.

– ISAIAH 40:28-31 (NIV)

How can you not feel empowered after reading this verse. Whew! Our God is amazing, unstoppable, and He can do all things. This is a great reminder: keep your faith and your hope in Him who can never fail! There are movies we all love that we can watch over and over again. Remember the Titans is one of those movies for me. The life lessons taught in that movie resonate and give me hope for our country's future. One of the characters recites this verse when trying to motivate the team to move past the racial divide they are facing. How ironic that we are facing such daunting times right now in 2020? This verse reminds us that no matter how tired we get of fighting the battles for justice, peace and equality, if we seek Him first, He will indeed renew our strength.

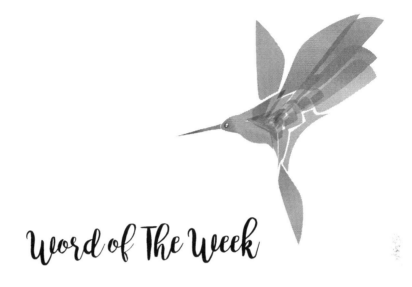

Word of The Week

---- **UNSTOPPABLE** ----

"Unstoppable" means impossible to stop or prevent. God's power is unstoppable. It cannot be thwarted, and when He is at work, no one and nothing can stop His will. What challenge or obstacle are facing in your life right now that is making you feel weary? Let this verse be a reminder that all you have to do is call on Him to see you through. He will give you the strength you need to push through.

Shall we Pray?

Magnificent and merciful Father we are forever in awe of you. Your strength and power carry us through all the days of our life. Be with us Lord and instill in us a spirit of strength and truth. Help us to understand the power in your name. All we need to do is call on the name of the Lord when we are weak and you are with us. You have all the answers to our questions and the missing pieces to our puzzles. Even when it doesn't make sense or look right in our eyes we trust the process and know that you will sustain us through it all. Grace us with your mercy and see us through our challenges. We are careful to give you all the praise and honor. We love and magnify your name – amen.

Listen to your heart

- I feel: _____
- I need: _____
- I forgive: _____
- I celebrate: _____
- I release: _____
- I trust: _____

The best thing about this week was

_____
_____

Me time – self care commitment

_____
_____
_____

I was grateful for:

_____
_____
_____
_____
_____
_____

Set Your Mind Free

Just Imagine

Week forty-two:
And we know that in all things God works for the good of those who love him, who have been called according to his purpose.

- ROMANS 8:28 (NIV)

- This one can sometimes be a hard one to digest. All things, Lord? Really, all things? Yes, the verse says all things, and even when we can't see the resolution or how God is going to work out some of our toughest challenges and obstacles, we must trust and know that He would not bring us into anything He is not capable of bringing us out of. There is purpose even in our pain. I can remember several years ago interviewing for a role I felt I was not only qualified for but that I deserved. I had worked hard, my results and performance exceeded the goals that had been set, and I had paid my dues, right? Wrong. The job went to another qualified candidate, but it was not me. It was a hard pill to swallow because I could not find fault in my process. The feedback I received was positive, they had just gone in a different direction. To say I was unhappy is an understatement. I was downright bitter, and it made me rethink what I was even doing in this organization. Clearly, they didn't see or appreciate my value. It was a rough time for me, but when I look back over that time in my life, I see so much purpose in the lessons I needed to learn. I can look back and see that the role really was not what I wanted and that I would not have been fulfilled. Yes, I would have had the title, but I would not be able to do the things I truly enjoyed about my job, the things that are truly my gift. There were other things God needed me to see and learn along my journey, and He then elevated me to the position He had chosen specifically for me!

Word of The Week

PURPOSE

Purpose is the reason for which something is done or created or why something exists. There is purpose in everything we encounter along our journey. We have to trust that God's plans and His timing are indeed the best plans. Create a list of valuable lessons gained through some of your toughest times. Reflect on your growth.

Shall we Pray?

Lord we need you. We can be so impatient at times and want what we want even though it may not be what is best for us. We are so quick to create our "plans" when in reality it is you who is in charge. This life is a gift but you never said it would be easy. Give us the courage and the strength to move through it all with grace and humility. Allow us to lay down our pride when necessary and master the lesson you are seeking to teach us. You are adding to our tool belt so that we can achieve the plan and purpose you placed us here for. When that happens we will be walking in our strength and grace. Our faith and trust is in you. We love you and we honor you – amen.

listen to your heart

- I feel: _____
- I need: _____
- I forgive: _____
- I celebrate: _____
- I release: _____
- I trust: _____

The best thing about this week was

_____
_____

Me time—self care commitment

_____
_____

I was grateful for:

_____
_____
_____
_____
_____
_____

It's time to daydream

Let your
Mind Soar

Week forty-three:

May the God of hope fill you with all joy and peace as you trust in him, so that you may overflow with hope by the power of the Holy Spirit.

– ROMANS 15:13 (NIV)

Some days, you just have to stop and take a moment to allow the Holy Spirit to fill you—fill you with peace, love, understanding, and joy. We all have those moments when life drags us down, when it gets heavy, or we have a tough day ahead of us. I have come to truly treasure my quiet time with God. I try my best to start every day with a little chat with the Lord along with reading a daily devotional or Scripture. I also write in my gratitude journal. These practices ground me and put me in a great state of mind to begin my day. I find the days that I don't take these steps, I am a bit off and not at my best. Allow yourself to quiet your heart and mind and let Him take over.

Word of The Week

PERMEATE

Permeate means to spread throughout. I think most of us think of the word "permeate" in regards to food. The smell of breakfast cooking on Sunday morning or the wonderful aroma of fresh-baked cookies during the holidays. Well, God's love permeates our hearts and minds in the same way. Allow the goodness of God in your life to permeate your heart and watch your entire mood lift!

Shall we Pray?

Oh heavenly Father, we come to you today first giving you our thanks and secondly asking you to take a hold of our hearts and our minds. Your spirit is real and it lives within each of us. We get so caught up in our day to day that we forget to let you in. When we do we our spirit is always calmed and our mind at peace. Please be with us this week as we dedicate ourselves to seeking quiet time with you. Time where we allow the distractions of our day to be placed on hold and we focus on hearing your voice. Thank you for loving us and for sending you only son to save us. We lift your name on high, amen.

Listen to your heart

- I feel: _____
- I need: _____
- I forgive: _____
- I celebrate: _____
- I release: _____
- I trust: _____

The best thing about this week was

_____
_____

Me time - self care commitment

_____
_____
_____

I was grateful for:

_____
_____
_____
_____
_____
_____

Set Your Mind Free

Just Imagine

Week forty-four:

For I am convinced that neither death nor life, neither angels nor demons, neither the present nor the future, nor any powers, neither height nor depth, nor anything else in all creation, will be able to separate us from the love of God that is in Christ Jesus our Lord.

– ROMANS 8:38-39 (NIV)

– There is nothing we can do to make God stop loving us—it's just that simple. It is the true definition of unconditional love. It's agape love, and it is indeed a selfless gift. I think we as humans believe we love one another unconditionally, but we have our own blind biases and judgements that get in the way of us truly loving and accepting each other for who and what we are. One of my favorite anonymous quotes is "Every time I judge someone else, I reveal an unhealed part of myself." Every day I strive to be more like God and love unconditionally.

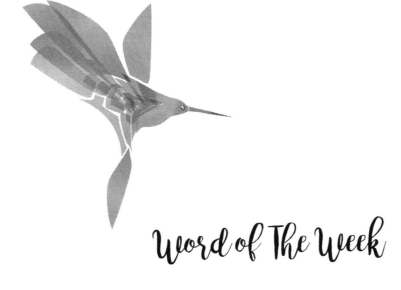

Word of The Week

UNCONDITIONAL

This kind of love is not subject to any conditions. We all say we love unconditionally, but do we really? Who do you share and offer unconditional love to on a regular basis? What are some ways you can strive to show the love and light of God to everyone you encounter?

Shall we Pray?

My sovereign Lord, we are so undeserving of your love, yet you offer your promise of everlasting life if we just believe. What an unselfish love for those you know will fail you every day. We are far from perfect but perfect in your sight and it is a gift we can never repay. You have shown us the example of love. You teach us that love is an action word and not a noun. Please give us the courage and the strength to be deliberate in our actions. Help us to do all things in love. We ask this prayer in your mighty and matchless name. Amen.

listen to your heart

- I feel: _____

- I need: _____

- I forgive: _____

- I celebrate: _____

- I release: _____

- I trust: _____

The best thing about this week was

_____

_____

Me time—self care commitment

_____

_____

I was grateful for:

_____

_____

_____

_____

_____

It's time to daydream

Let your Mind Soar

Week forty-five:

So that Christ may dwell in your hearts through faith. And I pray that you, being rooted and established in love, may have power, together with all the Lord's holy people, to grasp how wide and long and high and deep is the love of Christ, and to know this love that surpasses knowledge that you may be filled to the measure of all the fullness of God. Now to him who is able to do immeasurably more than all we ask or imagine, according to his power that is at work within us, to him be glory in the church and in Christ Jesus throughout all generations, for ever and ever! Amen.

- EPHESIANS 3:17-21

This has long been one of my all-time favorite verses. I am just in awe of His magnificence and His undying love for us. When God answers our prayers, the answer is always better than we could imagine. You just can't out-give or out-bless Him. Even though the answer may not come the way we expect, the answer is always on time and often better than what we had prayed for. I have learned to change my prayers to say, "If not this Lord than better than this." He never disappoints and always gives us exactly what we need. In 2018, I made a list of 30 things that would blow my mind if they happened. Things I knew only God could do. I prayed over the list and believed He would answer and He did. Not all 30 things were answered but enough of the list was and I knew it was only through Him that it was possible. A few examples were improving my credit score by over 200 points, refinancing my home, paying off debt, receiving a promotion, the healing of broken relationships, and spiritual growth. Not one of those things was within my power. God's hand was in it all.

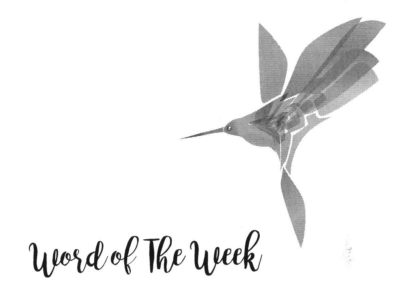

Word of The Week

ABUNDANCE

Abundance is prosperity—plentifulness of the good things of life. God truly wants the very best for us. He wants to give us our hearts' desires. What are you believing God for today? What abundance are you seeking in your life? Do you trust that He will give you above and beyond your greatest expectations?

Shall we Pray?

Oh heavenly Father, your word tells us to pray boldly. That you are never taken aback by our prayers or our hearts desires. Bold prayers honor you and you honor bold prayers. If our prayers aren't impossible to us they are actually insulting to you. You have shown us that you will do exceedingly and abundantly above all that we can think or ask and we must accept that as truth. Allow that to sink deep into our souls so that we move past the doubt, the stress and the fear and just focus on believing in you. You are mighty, magnificent and righteous. We thank you and we honor you. Amen

Listen to your heart

- I feel: _____
- I need: _____
- I forgive: _____
- I celebrate: _____
- I release: _____
- I trust: _____

The best thing about this week was

_____

_____

Me time—self care commitment

_____

_____

_____

I was grateful for:

_____

_____

_____

_____

_____

_____

Set Your Mind Free

Just Imagine

Week forty-six:

Be strong and courageous. Do not be afraid or terrified because of them, for the LORD your God goes with you; he will never leave you nor forsake you.

DEUTERONOMY 31:6

What immediately comes to mind when I read this verse is the battle is not yours; it's the Lord's, and no weapon formed against us shall prosper. No matter who or what we are dealing with, the Lord is always on our side, leading, guiding, and protecting us! There is nothing we should fear because our Lord goes before us. Whenever I am apprehensive about a situation, this scripture runs through my mind. I should fear absolutely nothing. The Lord is always present and in my corner. From difficult conversations and demanding deadlines to family challenges, we must remember that He goes before us in all things and is always making a way.

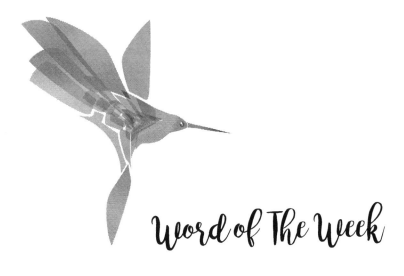

Word of The Week

WARRIOR

Do you recognize the hedge of protection around you on a daily basis? There are so many things God protects us from on a daily basis. We are truly unaware. The car accidents we could have been in as we rush to work, the phone call you stopped to take that may have prevented you remembering to turn off the fire on the stove. All these little things we take for granted. What has God protected you from recently? Make Psalm 91 a part of your reading this week.

Shall we Pray?

Oh Lord our Lord how excellent is thy name in all the earth. We come to you today so grateful for your warrior mentality and the many ways you protect us from dangers seen and unseen. It is by your grace that we move so freely through our days seemingly without a care in the world. We thank you so much for guiding us and guarding us. You keep us and assist us in getting out of our own way. As we approach another week we step into it with boldness knowing who has our back. There is no situation too big for you to conquer. Be with us as we fight our battles and help us to always give you the honor and the glory. Amen.

listen to your heart

- I feel: _____
- I need: _____
- I forgive: _____
- I celebrate: _____
- I release: _____
- I trust: _____

The best thing about this week was

_____

_____

Me time—self care commitment

_____

_____

I was grateful for:

_____

_____

_____

_____

_____

_____

It's time to daydream

Let your
Mind Soar

Week forty-seven:
Peace I leave with you; my peace I give you. I do not give to you as the world gives. Do not let your hearts be troubled and do not be afraid.

. – JOHN 14:27 (NIV)

God is not an indian giver – He is a promise keeper and His Word is true. The world will disappoint us and fall short of it's promises, but His word remains the truth! My grandmother told me years ago that I would live a life of disappointment because I placed too high of an expectation on people. She told me people are human; they will disappoint you. Place your trust in the one you can trust completely: God. As a child, I heard her but didn't quite understand. I get it now—through life's tribulations and the disappointment of others, I now know what she means. As humans, we will fail and we will sin. We are far from perfect, and the only one who is perfect is our Lord and Savior. Place you trust in Him; you can never go wrong.

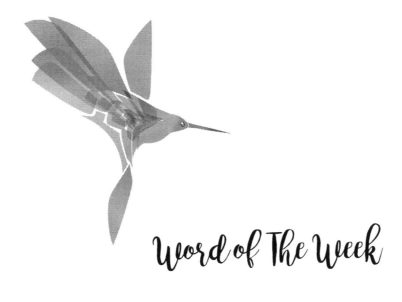

Word of The Week

AUTHENTICITY

Authenticity is the quality of being genuine, real, and transparently true. God is who He says He is; how can we emulate this level of authenticity in our daily lives? Don't you want to be known for your integrity and authenticity? This is something I strive for on a daily basis.

Shall we Pray?

Lord you see us for who and what we are. You accept and love us in spite of ourselves and we experience such a sense of freedom because of your unconditional love for us. We seek to live a life of authenticity. To walk in our truth and to embrace all parts of us knowing we are a work in progress. Help us to emulate your genuine heart for love. To be more like our heavenly father in all we do. We know that not everyone will be accepting of the journey we are on and that is OK with us because we have our minds staid on you. We thank you for your example and for teaching us compassion, empathy, forgiveness and truth. Let this be a reciprocal and continuous lesson in our life as we shine the love and light of our creator in all we say and do. Amen.

Listen to your heart

- I feel: _____
- I need: _____
- I forgive: _____
- I celebrate: _____
- I release: _____
- I trust: _____

The best thing about this week was

_____
_____

Me time—self care commitment

_____
_____
_____

I was grateful for:

_____
_____
_____
_____
_____
_____

Set Your Mind Free

Just Imagine

Week forty-eight:
But seek first the kingdom of God and his righteousness, and all these things will be provided for you.

– MATTHEW 6:33 (CSB)

God first in all things. When we "seek" or pray to Him above all else, we will be guided in the right direction. God is above all things, all people, and all action. Until I've prayed about it, I can't take action. I have had so many experiences in my life where God showed me His provision. Working in the field of retail, I have seen my fair share of mergers. Every merger that I have been a part of gave us a time frame in which we would have our jobs and the choice to perhaps interview and move with the new merged organization. In two of the three situations, relocation was not an option for me. I had to figure out my new way and search for a job. I never panicked, and I believed that God would show me the way. I went to Him first and asked for His covering and guidance, and He saw me through. Sometimes you have to praise God in the hallway while waiting for Him to open the next door.

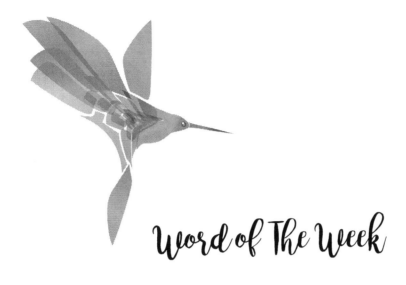

Word of The Week

PROVISION

This is the act of providing or supplying something for use. As parents, we provide for our children by having a safe place for them to live, giving them food to eat, and buying clothes to cover their bodies. We also give them love and affection so that they feel safe, secure, loved, and appreciated. God does all of this and more for us. How many ways does God continue to provide for you and your family?

Shall we Pray?

Dear Lord, there are not enough ways or enough times for us to say thank you. When we keep you as the true head of our households we cannot go wrong. Help us to live our lives in this manner. If we lead by example, our spouses, partners, children and friends will see what an amazing equation this truly is. Our goal is to always, always seek you first in all things. The big decisions and the little ones. This teaches us to truly hear your voice and it is what we so desire. Build our trust and our faith in you. You are the way, the truth and the light and we bow so humbly at your feet. Be with us this day and every day, amen.

listen to your heart

- I feel: _____
- I need: _____
- I forgive: _____
- I celebrate: _____
- I release: _____
- I trust: _____

The best thing about this week was

_____

_____

Me time — self care commitment

_____

_____

I was grateful for:

_____

_____

_____

_____

_____

_____

It's time to daydream

_____

_____

_____

_____

_____

_____

_____

_____

_____

_____

_____

_____

_____

_____

_____

_____

_____

Let your
Mind Soar

Week forty-nine:

Do not be anxious about anything, but in every situation, by prayer and petition, with thanksgiving, present your requests to God. And the peace of God, which transcends all understanding, will guard your hearts and your minds in Christ Jesus.

PHILIPPIANS 4:6-7 (NIV)

This is one of the first verses I memorized early in my faith walk and always go to when I catch myself worrying or becoming stressed. God knows our hearts and hears our cries. Take it to Him and allow His peace to surround you. It is a natural tendency to worry or fret over things that are important to you. Some of us are true worriers and allow each and every thing in our life to cause that horrible feeling of anxiousness. My mom is a natural worrier, and I vowed I would not repeat that behavior. It is hard; I am a control freak, so knowing things are not going to go as planned most days is a hard fact to digest. My outlook now, however, has changed. When I feel the worry coming on, I immediately start praying. I ask God to take it from me and I know that He will. I also don't question the outcome of things as much anymore, realizing His ways are not ours; it won't always make sense to me right away and sometimes not at all. I am a work in progress for sure.

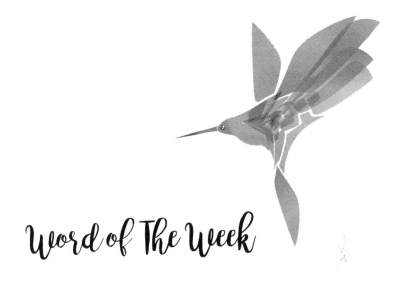

Word of The Week

COMFORT

Comfort is the easing or alleviation of a person's feelings of grief or distress. Reflect on this verse any time this week when you find yourself feeling overwhelmed or stressed. Allow it to give you peace

Shall we Pray?

Lord, there is such power in the act of prayer. We ask you Lord to help us become prayer warriors – always seeking prayer above all else. Give us the confidence and resolve only a talk with you can bring. You equip us with tools Lord to use as we walk along our journey. Prayer is imperative and we ask that you be with us as we work to incorporate it into our day. We are so happy to give you all the praise and all the glory. Amen

Listen to your heart

- I feel: _____
- I need: _____
- I forgive: _____
- I celebrate: _____
- I release: _____
- I trust: _____

The best thing about this week was

_____

_____

Me time—self care commitment

_____

_____

_____

I was grateful for:

_____

_____

_____

_____

_____

_____

Set Your Mind Free

Just Imagine

Week fifty:
Charm is deceptive, and beauty is fleeting; but a woman who fears the Lord is to be praised.

– PROVERBS 31:30 (NIV)

True beauty is not in the face; beauty is a light in the heart, an illumination of your soul. Have you ever met a physically beautiful woman or handsome man who was just not attractive to you in any way? I have, and it was because of their negative or nasty attitude or outlook on life. Or perhaps they spoke poorly of another person, were filled with critiques and gossip. This type of behavior, the kind of behavior not pleasing to God, can diminish the outward beauty of a person very quickly. There are also those people you meet who are so genuine and kind and who have beautiful hearts that their outward beauty grows. I tell my daughter often that while I see her outward beauty, I am most in awe of the beauty of her heart. She is kind, loving, and compassionate. These qualities are irreplaceable and outshine physical beauty any day.

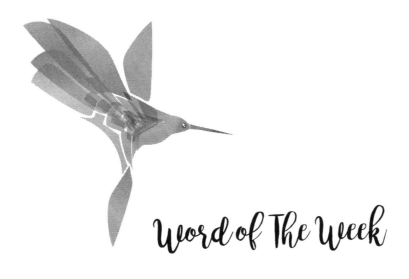

Word of The Week

INNER BEAUTY

Inner beauty is the personality of a person, including their mind, soul, and inner values and characteristics. Our society places so much value on our outward appearance. We tend to lose focus on the inner work that is so necessary. Building the kingdom of God is not based on physical appearances but on possessing the heart and love of God. Spend time this week working on the beauty that is not seen but felt.

Shall we Pray?

Our most magnificent Father, as we approach a new week we ask you to give us a new mindset. A mindset that does not focus on our physical appearances but one that focuses on our heart. Help us to be the best version of ourself, to strive to be a Proverbs 31 woman who has the heart of God. We know that we are far from perfect. We want others to admire the beauty of our spirit and not our physical beauty. Allow the fruit's of the spirit to shine brightly to all we encounter. We love you, we honor you, we praise your holy name. Amen.

listen to your heart

- I feel: _____
- I need: _____
- I forgive: _____
- I celebrate: _____
- I release: _____
- I trust: _____

The best thing about this week was

_____

_____

Me time—self care commitment

_____

_____

I was grateful for:

_____

_____

_____

_____

_____

_____

It's time to daydream

Let your
Mind Soar

Week fifty-one:
For the Spirit God gave us does not make us timid, but gives us power, love and self-discipline.

- 2 TIMOTHY 1:7 (NIV)

Just because we are Christians does not mean we are timid or that we should allow people to walk over us. His spirit lives within us and empowers us in all we do. Walk in great power and authority each and every day, for you are a child of the Most High. I am sure we can all remember a time when we had to assert ourselves—when we had to stand up and take charge of a situation or circumstance that was potentially putting us in a bad position. When I first got into management, I was a lot younger than the majority of the people I was managing. It was intimidating at times because I knew many of them had a lot more experience than I did, but I had been placed in this role for a reason. I at times felt unequipped, which shook my confidence, but I had to trust that not only had my employer put me there for a reason, but God had put me there for a purpose. Seek Him in all things and you cannot go wrong. He gives us all we need to accomplish what is before us.

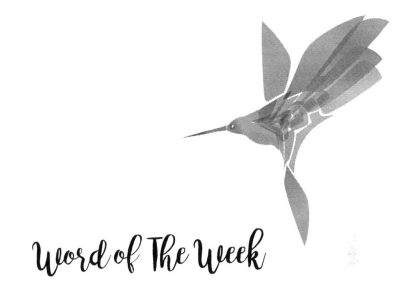

Word of The Week

EQUIP

Equipping someone means preparing them mentally for a particular situation or task. Allow yourself to feel the power of God working in and through you every day. You are empowered by His grace; walk in confidence in all you do. He equips us for the tasks, trials, and tribulations along our journey.

Shall we Pray?

Lord we come to you today asking you to equip us with what we need this week to accomplish the tasks, projects and assignments you have given us. You have chosen us to get it done and we always want to do our best. When we falter or have our moments where we question our abilities pour forth your love so that we can push through. We are your children and we do not walk in fear. Help us not to be intimidated by anything or anyone. Your grace and mercy sustain us and follow us all the days of our lives.

Listen to your heart

- I feel: _____
- I need: _____
- I forgive: _____
- I celebrate: _____
- I release: _____
- I trust: _____

The best thing about this week was

_____
_____

Me time - self care commitment

_____
_____
_____

I was grateful for:

_____
_____
_____
_____
_____
_____

Set Your Mind Free

Just Imagine

Week fifty-two:
""The LORD bless you and keep you; the LORD make his face shine on you and be gracious to you; the LORD turn his face toward you and give you peace"

- NUMBERS 6:24-26

I always feel so refreshed and bolstered at the end of a church service when I hear the pastor close with these words. I feel like I am ready to take on whatever may come my way. Know that you are covered: covered by His blood, His grace, and His mercy. My heart is full of gratitude. This verse reminds me that we are a reflection of God's light and His love. It is truly our responsibility as Christians to shine this love and light on others. The best compliment someone can give me is to tell me they see the love of God in me. I know then that I am doing His will.

Word of The Week

COVERED

To cover is to place something over a person in order to conceal or protect it. God's love for us is a covering. It is precious and given to us freely just because He loves us that much. He wants to bear the brunt of our burdens and protect us from the hurts of the world. How has God covered you in this season? What has He revealed to you during this time?

Shall we Pray?

Heavenly Father, you constantly cover and protect us. As we travel the road before us we ask that you continue to grant us the grace you give us so freely each and every day. As your children, we are privileged. Your blood is running through our veins and we are truly descendants of the king. Help us to remember this as we approach this life we are leading. It should sustain and strengthen us in all we do and in all we encounter. We ask you to continue to be with us. Your love is the greatest of all gifts. We pray this and other blessings in your mighty and matchless name. Amen.

listen to your heart

- I feel: _____
- I need: _____
- I forgive: _____
- I celebrate: _____
- I release: _____
- I trust: _____

The best thing about
this week was

_____
_____

Me time — self care
commitment

_____
_____
_____

I was grateful
for:

_____
_____
_____
_____
_____
_____

It's time to
daydream

_____

_____

_____

_____

_____

_____

_____

_____

_____

_____

_____

_____

_____

_____

Let your
Mind Soar

Made in the USA
Columbia, SC
25 November 2020